To BANAA

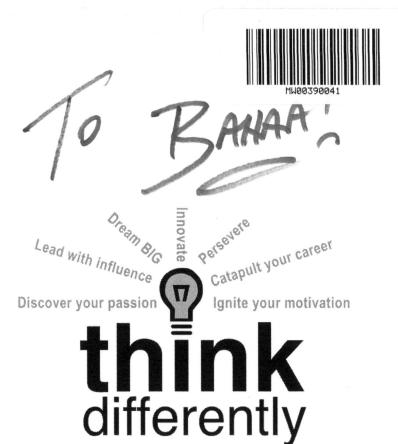

Dream BIG Innovate Persevere
Lead with influence Catapult your career
Discover your passion Ignite your motivation

think
differently

— Kevin Snyder

As you read,
tweet and post your thoughts to
#ThinkDifferently and @KevinCSnyder.

Bulk rate discounted purchasing is available by contacting the publishing coordinator listed below or by contacting the author. Bulk book orders over 100 in quantity will contain a customized first page with company logo and welcome message.

Edited by Lee Heinrich
Layout and Design by CSinclaire Write-Design
Published by Write Way Publishing Company
www.WriteWayPublishingCompany.com
"We help aspiring authors become published authors!"

For additional information:
Dr. Kevin C. Snyder
www.KevinCSnyder.com
Kevin@KevinCSnyder.com
Follow Kevin on your social of choice @KevinCSnyder

Thank you for investing in yourself.

I believe this book, *Think Differently*, has landed in your hands because this coming year is destined to be the best year of your life. I believe you are ready to achieve more at a level far exceeding even your current expectations.

I wrote this book to be a catalyst for you. The leadership lessons and personal life stories you will read about are designed to equip and empower you to *think differently* about your challenges and any adversity you face. They are also designed to help you identify your passions and envision new possibility.

Since the first publication of this book, I've recently expanded content, refreshed the formatting, and added reflection opportunities for you at the conclusion of each chapter.

I wish for you a *think differently* mindset. Congratulations in advance, and I look forward to hearing about your achievements to come!

Receive a daily motivational quote by downloading my app on your phone/iPad. Simply go to your app store and search for "KevinCSnyder."

Download FREE
leadership resources

T hank you for investing your valuable time to read *Think Differently*! Since we're of "like mind," I'd like to send you a special free link to download many of my leadership resources. Simply visit **www.KevinCSnyder.com** and enter your email address when the opt-in image appears. You'll receive an immediate response with the special link.

After you finish reading *Think Differently*, please share a testimonial and help spread the positive message of this book to others! I'd love to read your thoughts. Submit your testimonial on Amazon.com following these easy steps:

#1: *Visit **www.Amazon.com***

#2: *In the Amazon search bar, type "Think Differently and Kevin Snyder" so that you find this book. Click on it!*

#3: *Scroll down and click on "Write a Customer Review." Add your review and submit it!*

#4: *After writing your review, email me at **Kevin@KevinCSnyder.com** and I will reply with an additional special link for FREE stuff!*

Note: Although Amazon.com is preferred, you can also visit my website to make book purchases, leave reviews (**www.KevinCSnyder.com**) or contact me directly for bulk discount orders (**Kevin@KevinCSnyder.com**)

A quick nugget about the author

As a struggling teenager who battled depression and being arrested, Kevin experienced several turning points that guided him to pursue a speaking and writing career in personal development.

Kevin holds a Doctorate degree in Educational Leadership and has worked for several institutions of higher education, most recently as the Dean of Students at High Point University.

Kevin now speaks to audiences all over the world ranging from high schools and colleges to corporate organizations and professional associations of all types. He's honored to have spoken to over 1,150 audiences in all 50 states and around the world on topics inclusive of leadership development, team empowerment, building highly performing cultures, and much more.

As a published author and professional speaker, Kevin also coaches aspiring authors and speakers to reach their writing and speaking goals.

Kevin is a Forbes magazine contributor, a sailboat charter captain, a certified skydiver, scuba diver, kiteboarding enthusiast, and most interestingly, a winner on television's most famous game show, *The Price Is Right!*

> "Our desires are uniquely planted within us for a reason. It's up to us whether we make them bloom." — *KEVIN C. SNYDER*

Dedicated to You ...

because you opened this book and have a desire

to make a difference in your life and the lives of others.

Here's to your life-changing year ahead.

— *Kevin*

P.S. *Take me with you on your journey reading this book. Tag me on social media with your thoughts* **@KevinCSnyder** *and/or use the hashtag* **#ThinkDifferently** *to share any quotes or messages that also resonate with you. You can also send me an email at* **Kevin@KevinCSnyder.com**. *I'd love to connect and hear from you while you're reading this book.*

Contents

Think
Differently

**"Insanity is doing the same thing over and over
again and yet expecting a different result."**
— *ALBERT EINSTEIN*

Think differently—that's the fundamental concept
of this book. Thinking differently is also an essential
concept for living a successful and—more importantly—a fulfilling life.

Each of us has absolute control over one thing: our
thoughts. The way we think determines how we feel, and
how we feel dictates how we act. Our thoughts manifest an
outcome, and our actions and behaviors can be changed
at any moment simply by recognizing the power of our
thoughts *in that moment*.

No matter where you've been or where you are in

life, your "today" depends on you. And your future, as well, depends on the choices you make, or don't make, today. This book will help you get excited about new possibility.

• *THE PAST DOES NOT EQUAL THE FUTURE!* •

The most important day of your life is always "today." Why? This day won't be repeated, so you might as well make the most of it! Would you like this day of your life to be different, to have more passion and purpose than ever before, to live beyond what might be frustrating or limiting you right now, and to gain newfound happiness and life direction? The first step is in realizing the importance of having a *think differently* mindset. Only by thinking differently can we grow and live to our most full potential.

We all have a story. This book is mine. Each chapter is a different lesson I've learned about life and leadership—most of them the hard way. It took years for me to finally understand how my struggles developed my strengths. How my mistakes were actually teachable moments waiting for me to learn the lesson. As I thought differently about my regrets, I realized all my setbacks were setups for future success!

On the next page is one of the leadership activities I share with audiences I'm presenting to all over the world.

Look at the nine dots on the next page.

Now, with your finger or a pencil, try to connect all nine dots with four straight lines, keeping your finger or pencil on the page at all times.

Do not continue reading until you've spent at least

one minute trying to connect all nine dots. *(Imagine Jeopardy theme music here!)*

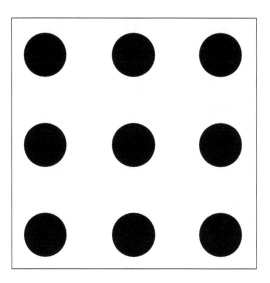

Were you successful at connecting all nine dots with four straight lines while keeping your finger on the paper?

If so, congratulations (especially if you have never seen this challenge before)!

If you were not able to connect all nine dots, you are not alone. I incorporate this activity into all my presentations because it's the starting block to understanding the power of a *think differently* mindset. To date I have spoken in front of more than 1,150 audiences all over the world and among all those, only three people (of those who had not previously seen this exercise) were able to complete it successfully.

Turn the page for the solution.

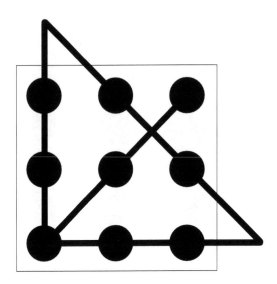

As you can see, in order to complete the task, you must think "outside the box." You have likely heard this expression dozens of times before, but unfortunately, most of us do not understand the importance of this concept applied in our lives.

I believe that in order to achieve what we truly want and desire in life, we must *think differently*—outside the box. Only then will we fully experience life and accomplish our dreams to their full potential.

"Inside the box" is where we all feel most comfortable. It's what we're used to and what we know, so it's natural to want to stay there. It constitutes—here's another familiar phrase—our "comfort zone."

Each of us has a comfort zone, and everyone's comfort zone is unique. On one spectrum, some folks have such expansive comfort zones that they readily welcome a challenge, take risk, and seem to be able to try anything new without any hesitation. On the contrary, other peoples' comfort zones are smaller so that they become uncomfortable with change, anxious about taking risk and extremely resistant to doing anything different. And of course, there are all ranges of "comfort zones" in between.

But the one constant on this wide-ranging spectrum is that a person who stays too long within the boundaries of his or her comfort zone stops growing. They stop stretching. They stop pushing themselves to try new things. They become comfortable.

Seeds of complacency are unintentionally planted and weeds of routine begin to grow, taking precedence over finding new opportunity. This explains why so many people ultimately feel stuck and unhappy. They are enduring their life on a daily basis instead of living it with passion and purpose.

"The only limitations we have are the ones we mentally place there."
— FRANKLIN D. ROOSEVELT, FORMER U.S. PRESIDENT

Yes, we all would prefer to stay inside our comfort zone. It is where we feel safe. It is where we feel in control. We guard its borders jealously, usually without even being aware of it.

But the paradigm to understand is that our comfort zone also limits us. By not stepping outside our comfort zone to try new things and experience new approaches to life, we are not challenging ourselves to live our full potential.

More importantly, we stop living and start enduring. And I don't believe any of us are here on this planet to endure life. I believe we are here to prosper. We are here to make this world a better place. We are here to enjoy, appreciate, and relish in the extraordinary opportunities this world provides for us. We are designed to live with purpose and help others do the same.

But we have to acknowledge comfort zones in order to know where ours are. Only by recognizing a comfort zone exists within each of us can we push beyond it at times—even when it feels uncomfortable. Pushing through our comfort zone feels uncomfortable because we're trying something new. It means we're confronting the status quo. It means, we're growing.

> **"Everything you want in life is just outside your comfort zone."**
> — *JACK CANFIELD*

Maybe you've never noticed this, but rubber bands never regain their original shape once they've been substantially stretched. They stretch farther and farther as more tension and pull is placed on them, and gradually, they can encompass much more than in their original state.

Like a rubber band, comfort zones also expand and shrink depending on how they are pulled or pushed. As you move "outside the box" to try and experience new things, as you test the boundaries of your mental and physical strength, and as you push through any uncomfortability, your comfort zone expands as well. In this way, your mind is akin to a rubber band!

"The most successful people have said their greatest success comes just one step beyond the point at which defeat had overtaken them."
— *NAPOLEON HILL*, THINK AND GROW RICH

It is a natural and intrinsic quality of human nature to avoid discomfort and pain. Most of us subconsciously avoid feeling uncomfortable at all costs.

Despite this very human tendency, I suggest and challenge you to change your mental association with this feeling of being uncomfortable; instead of avoiding it, consider embracing it. When you consistently are open to taking a risk, trying new approaches, and expanding your comfort zone, you will slowly become more *comfortable* feeling *uncomfortable*. Only then will you know you are stretching your limits and challenging your personal boundaries and limitations.

"You only find your limits by going beyond them."
— *ROGER BANNISTER*

So, in the spirit of helping you take your life to the next level, think about what makes you feel uncomfortable.

- What is it?
- Is it a thing?
- A situation?
- An environment?

Identify something that makes you feel uncomfortable and write about it below.

_____

_____

_____

_____

_____

_____

_____

_____

_____

_____

_____

_____

_____

_____

_____

_____

_____

_____

Now reflect on what you wrote. What about it makes you feel uncomfortable?

Is it fear? Uncertainty? Or is it that you're not sure what you want? Maybe you know what you want, but you don't feel you deserve it. Maybe you don't feel prepared. Maybe you've never done it before. Maybe it requires some risk.

All your feelings are legitimate, but you must identify what makes you uncomfortable and be aware why. Awareness is the first step towards a new beginning. Think about it this way—if it's new to you or if it's going to require some type of risk to do it or confront it, you *should* feel uncomfortable. But remember that feeling slightly uncomfortable is part of the success equation. Don't let that feeling stop you. Once you embrace that feeling as part of the journey and take one simple, small step toward it, you'll be shocked how that feeling of uncomfortability goes away!

And whether you realize it or not, a mindset of comfortability is what keeps us locked inside our comfort zone—thus limiting our personal growth.

Think about the advice you would give to your child— or any young child—if they asked you about how to live life to its fullest. I would imagine a common theme in most people's responses would be for the child to "reach for the stars" and "pursue something that makes them happy." Yes?

We need to follow that same advice we would give to a child. And not just today, but every single day of our lives!

Einstein said, *"Imagination is the preview to life's coming attractions."* In other words, *if you can envision your goal*, you can accomplish it. What's waiting is for you to identify what that goal looks like. If fear is holding you back, the first step you *must* take is confronting that fear. This will require pushing yourself outside your comfort zone. Recognize that "feeling uncomfortable" is a requirement for moving toward your dream and achieving your goals. Only *you* can break through your personal mindset barriers.

One of the common denominators of success that I have discovered through my research on extraordinary leaders and organizations is that these individuals feel comfortable being uncomfortable. They know that uncomfortability only results from continually pushing, paddling, and trying new things. They constantly look for new waves to surf. They understand that complacency is a dream killer.

> **To watch my TEDx talk titled "The Ripple Effect: How Extraordinary Leaders Think Differently," visit http://kevincsnyder.com/free-stuff (17 min)**

When you take that *first step*—and I'm here to tell you, it is an incredible feeling—it's a rush beyond explanation. Already with just one step, you are on your way to manifesting something new and better in your life. You will discover a brave new sensation of accomplishment, and you will want to apply this fundamental concept of stepping out of your comfort zone to reach even more goals in your life.

Of course, it will take time, effort, and determination to solidify this neuro-association, so understand it will not happen overnight. Like a toddler learning to walk, you will need to take baby steps to change your mental focus. Even if you fall down and feel like you can't continue, you will need to force yourself to try again and again—and even then again. Remember, it's not how many times you fall, it's how many times you get back up. And it's nearly impossible to beat someone who never quits. So your biggest competitor is going to be you. I'm confident though, that this book will help you realize how to champion yourself in ways like never before!

Reflect back on when you first learned to ride a bicycle. Maybe you started out with training wheels, like most young riders do. But even after you left the training wheels behind, did you successfully ride on every attempt after that? More likely, you fell down once in a while and maybe even hurt yourself. But you got back up. You kept riding. Soon you were riding that bike like second nature, possibly even taking your hands off the handlebar!

> **"You cannot change your destination overnight, but you can alter your direction." — *JIM ROHN***

Another example is one's own body. Look at how a person builds muscle and becomes physically healthy. Do we simply build muscle overnight or does this activity require mental and physical discipline over a period of time?

You have the power to literally alter your physical appearance by taking action and changing your diet and exercise routine. Granted, some people seem to be more genetically gifted than others in this area, but it is simply fascinating to know we can alter our body's physical shape and appearance when we *decide* to. This process takes time and requires dedication and sacrifice. Once one step is accomplished, it's easier to take the next one, and you feel great about the achievement.

I've mentioned only a few simple analogies of how anyone can change an outcome by *thinking differently*—outside the box.

We have grown up hearing this cliché, but most people think of it as an occasional problem-solving strategy—not a life-changing one. Few ever consider applying it to their personal lives. In fact, most people give no thought to, and therefore have no understanding or appreciation for, the power of expanding *comfort zones* and *thinking differently*. That is also why most of society is content with being mediocre.

I do not write that statement as a criticism. My personal definition of mediocre is "status quo" or an acceptance of "being average." And there is nothing wrong with being average.

But "being average" is not what most people want. Think about it. Is your purpose in life to be average? Would you want your children to grow up average?

I personally do not believe my purpose in life is to be average. I choose and aspire every day to live my life exceptionally with passion and purpose. I know I am here for an extraordinary reason, even if there are times I'm trying to identify what that reason is. If I don't continually grow and *think differently*, average sets in.

I feel there are two ways to combat average. One is by taking different action. Action is a choice, and embracing it is the best way to tackle inaction! Even if action intimidates us, we'll always be glad we took action afterwards.

The second is by appreciating what you *do have* and what's in front of you right now. For example, there are moments of each day when I just relax and take a break. There are moments when I'm on my sailboat that nothing else matters except me and the wind. When I'm "in the moment," I'm appreciating the present and also feeling grateful for the benefits I've earned and received from pushing myself prior. As you'll learn in a later section, gratitude is extremely important to living a fulfilled life and fostering a successful, *think differently* mindset.

So, are you ready to combat average? Do you desire to help others move beyond average as well? If you wish to live your life in an "above average" fashion and you feel destined for more in your life and to help others achieve the same, then this book has arrived in your life at the absolute perfect time.

• ROGER BANNISTER •

It was once considered impossible that a human could run one mile in less than four minutes. That was before Roger Bannister appeared on the scene.

On May 16, 1954, at Iffley Road track in Oxford, England, Bannister, an amazing athlete, ran a mile in less than four minutes, accomplishing what truly had been considered beyond human capability.

The real surprise, though, was that shortly after Bannister's record-breaking accomplishment, several other individuals also broke the same record. A year after that, even more followed. Since then, hundreds of athletes have run in Bannister's record-breaking footsteps.

In a world where none before Bannister had achieved—perhaps never even aspired to—such an accomplishment, how was it that, suddenly, the four-minute-mile record was being broken on a regular basis by numerous runners?

What was different between Bannister's landmark year and the year or years following? Was it training break-throughs? Technology? Shoes? Supplements?

Of course not. The sole reason others were able to break this record was because they now *knew* it could be done. They saw that it was possible because one person—Roger Bannister—had done it.

Bannister proved to the world that the four-min-ute mile was only a mindset. It was a mental limitation and boundary that he believed he could break through. He *thought differently* and courageously raced outside of the comfort zone that the "everyone" had decreed as truth.

So, for just a moment, let's make this about you. **Imagine** how amazing it feels to live with a *think differently* mindset like Roger Bannister—to live with such courage and conviction about your goals that anything you set your mind to achieve can, and will, become a reality. **Envision** a daily life where negative comments from naysayers just bounce right off you and motivate you further. Model being the Roger Bannister for others, by showing them what *is possible*. And by watching you, they will believe in a new realm of possibility. You will be an inspiration that changes lives. All you need to do is live with a *think differently* mindset.

Try this: **Identify** something you'd like to do that has never been done. Or perhaps think of something that you've always wanted to do but have never tried, or others have told you it cannot be done for some reason. Now **convince yourself** for one moment that you *can* do it. **Imagine** it really can be done but that it just hasn't been done—yet. Like Bannister, believe this barrier to accomplishment is just a mindset and a matter of time before you break through it too. Now **envision** the end result and achievement of breaking through that barrier that everyone else considers impassable and says cannot be done. **Watch** them smiling at you and clapping for you. **Listen** to their words of congratulations to you directly for doing what has never been done before. **Hear** them tell others how proud they are of you. **Feel** the satisfaction of accomplishing that breakthrough and proudly living your dream.

How does that accomplishment feel inside you? Do you feel empowered?

Before you even begin your journey working toward that goal, keep this feeling inside you. Expect that feeling to manifest. You'll be attracting that reality before you even begin, during the obstacles, and at every step along the way.

But this reality will be difficult to manifest if you haven't yet conditioned yourself with a *think differently* mindset. So, let's be mindful for just a moment. What limitations have you believed in up until now? What limitations have been placed *upon you* that you've believed in up until now? Are there reasons you have not moved forward? What has someone told you could not be done that you believed and, because of that belief, stopped trying to do? What societal traditions have you accepted—like everyone else—simply because no one so far has successfully challenged them?

The next time someone tells you something can't be done—or worse, that *you* cannot do it—remember this story about Roger Bannister. Roger did what the entire world said could *not* be done. And the moment he proved it could be done, he—one person—changed history. More importantly, he inspired others with a *think differently* mindset to do the same.

"We've never done it that way."

"That won't work."

When you hear words like these, just smile at that person and say, "Okay, thank you." Then proudly allow them to watch you do it.

"It always seems impossible until it's done."
— *NELSON MANDELA*

There are thousands of stories about people just like Roger Bannister. I speak about many of them in my leadership programs. But your story is no different. Like everyone, you have obstacles in your life. You feel alone at times. You have challenges and circumstances that are difficult to push through. At times, you wonder if anything really matters and are tempted to give up. It's tough to wake up sometimes. I get that. Respectfully, I've been there. I'm still there sometimes.

As you'll read in upcoming chapters, I battled depression when I was a teenager. I was diagnosed with an eating disorder called anorexia nervosa and nearly died. I considered suicide on multiple occasions. I've been arrested. I've had toxic relationships. I've been cheated on. I've had a horrible boss. I've worked in an office environment that sucked the energy right out of me. I've been laid off, and I've collected unemployment. I've had a bank account that went from six figures to overdraft. I've had a home foreclosed on. I've filed for bankruptcy. I've lived paycheck to paycheck. My dog was hit by a car and killed while I was away speaking and "my friend" keeping him never even apologized. My sister, brother, and father have all battled cancer. I battled imposter syndrome most of my early adult life, feeling that I wasn't good enough. Most of my relationships have failed.

But the good news, heck, the extraordinary news, is that those days are behind me. Those times in my life were devastating, and I would never want to repeat them. I wish I could forget some of them, but I can't. But because I'm aware of the importance and power of a *think differently* mindset, I don't run away from past mistakes any longer. I embrace them as lessons of wisdom because they've made me into who I am today. I couldn't do what I do today if those experiences hadn't led me to where I am.

I don't run away from current challenges either because I understand I must constantly challenge myself in order to grow. I must "walk my own talk" and push through my own comfort zones. I have conditioned my mind to see every frustration, limitation, and negative experience I am confronted by as an opportunity to learn something new. I'm still learning and growing. And as long as I'm breathing, I'll never stop. The journey always continues, because I am that journey. You are the journey as well.

In many ways, I'm no different than you. You see, it's how we think about challenges and our current circumstances that will either set us apart and inspire others—like Roger Bannister—or leave us floating in the ocean of status quo. As long as we continue to paddle against complacency and live with a *think differently* mindset, we'll not only be living up to our potential, but excelling and inspiring others to do the same.

I believe you are reading this book for a reason. I believe you have it in your hand for a reason. You are destined for greatness beyond your wildest imagination once you identify that reason and are willing to embrace a *think differently* mindset. By doing so, you will unleash a new power inside you, one that will be a catalyst sparking new enthusiasm and passion in your life. I'm honored to be part of your journey.

REMEMBER: I'd love to hear from you while you're reading this book. Take me with you on your journey and tag me on social media with your thoughts *@KevinCSnyder* and/ or use the hashtag *#ThinkDifferently* to share any quotes or messages that also resonate with you. You can also send me an email at Kevin@KevinCSnyder.com. I'd love to connect and hear from you while you're reading this book.

• JACK CANFIELD AND MARK VICTOR HANSEN •

W ho are these two individuals? Even if you don't recognize their names, you likely have heard of and possibly read volumes from their series of books.

Jack Canfield and Mark Victor Hansen are the co-editors and creators of *Chicken Soup for the Soul*, the most successful series of books ever published.

However, these books were not successful overnight and, in fact, the publishing of them was nearly a miracle. What most people do not know is that Jack Canfield and Mark Victor Hansen went to over one hundred publishers before someone finally thought their idea might be successful. They experienced over a hundred rejections before they finally heard a "yes!"

The publisher who said "yes" is the only publisher who mattered—and matters. Look now at how successful this series of books has become. It is imperative that you recognize that all it takes is one "yes" to make all the difference in your life as well.

What would have happened if Jack Canfield and Mark Victor Hansen had stopped after hearing so many "no" answers? Obviously, *Chicken Soup for the Soul* would not exist. But because they were determined and believed in their dream of publishing their book, they knew it was just a matter of time before someone would see the potential in their idea. In fact, they anticipated the frustration that would occur when some publishers would not like their idea. So, when the doors were shut in their faces, they were not surprised. They simply learned from each experience and moved on.

"An invincible determination
can accomplish anything."
— *JACK CANFIELD AND MARK VICTOR HANSEN*

How many steps will you take toward your dream or an idea in which others may or may not believe? Will you be like Jack Canfield and Mark Victor Hansen, or will you expect the easy route and stop when you hear your first "no"?

With a *think differently* mindset, you'll embrace that each "no" will be leading you to your "yes!" Because if it was easy, wouldn't everyone be doing it? You just need to want it bad enough not to quit. It's that simple.

IT COMES DOWN
TO ONE SIMPLE
THING:

**HOW BAD DO YOU
WANT IT?**

What do you want so badly that you won't quit? What is a desire that inspires you to do whatever is necessary to accomplish it? Write it below.

_____

_____

_____

_____

_____

_____

_____

_____

_____

_____

_____

_____

_____

_____

_____

_____

_____

Always remind yourself that by *thinking differently*, you could have the same success as Jack Canfield and Mark Victor Hansen. These two individuals are no better than you or I are; they simply are an example of possessing a *think differently* mindset!

Thinking like *Chicken Soup for the Soul* authors, how many attempts will you make to live your dream?

• MICHAEL JORDAN •

M ichael Jordan is one of the best basketball players in history:

- **NBA's Most Valuable Player** — 5 times
- **NBA Finals Most Valuable Player** — 6 times
- **Member of NBA Championship Team** — 6 times
- **All-Star** — 11 times
- **Slam-Dunk Champion in** 1987 and 1988
- **Earned 10 NBA Scoring titles**
- **Average of 31.5 points per game, setting an** NBA record
- **Made 25 game-winning shots**
- **Scored 50 or more points in 37 games**
- **Scored highest points in a regular season game** (69 points)

But did you know that Michael Jordan was actually cut from his high-school basketball team? Yes, one of the world's all-time greatest basketball players was once told he wasn't good enough.

What do you think he did when he got home from school that day after being cut from the team? Play video games? Complain and turn away from the sport he loved? Believe that he wasn't good enough?

Heck, no.

The first thing Michael did when he got home was practice. He knew he was better than the coach thought. In fact, he didn't believe for one second that he wasn't. For the next year, Jordan practiced constantly, shooting free throws and lay ups, getting better and better each day.

When tryouts came around the following year, he not only made the team, he played amazingly well. Later he was an outstanding player for the University of North Carolina at Chapel Hill. Then came the NBA, and the rest is simply history.

I share Jordan's story to showcase that it takes sacrifice, discipline, sweat, and sometimes even tears to achieve dreams and goals. Nothing worthwhile ever happens overnight. Yet, even knowing better, we often still expect it to.

The reason you and I know about Michael Jordan is because he *thought differently*. He knew he was better than his high school coach thought he was. He knew he would break records and be an amazing basketball star. If Jordan had taken his coach's opinion at face value, he probably would never have persisted in pursuit of his goals or achieved the athletic records he attained. And we most likely would never have heard of him. What mattered to Michael Jordan was what *he* thought of *himself*, not what anyone *else* thought of him.

Michael Jordan used the disbelief of others to empower himself to become a better basketball player. I believe he is who he is *because* he was cut from the basketball team. That experience gave him his motivation, and he leveraged it to his advantage. As a result, he became an extraordinary basketball player.

Has anyone ever told you that you were not good

at something? Did you believe them? Do you really need someone else's approval to live your dream? Or can you find in yourself a motivation and attitude similar to Michael Jordan's so that you can pursue your desires without waiting for the world's permission or approval?

The next time someone doubts your abilities or says you cannot do something, remember Michael Jordan's story and *think differently*. Smile at your critics, then proudly let them watch as you climb to the top of your game.

Be like Mike.

> ***To watch Michael Jordan's incredible***
> ***Hall of Fame acceptance speech, visit***
> ***http://kevincsnyder.com/free-stuff*** **(23 min)**

Imagine you are Michael Jordan and you have the basketball. If you do not shoot it, what are the chances of the ball going into the hoop?

That's right. ZERO.

If you do not take a shot, there is a one hundred percent chance the ball will not go through the hoop. When you take your shot, you at least have a chance. You may not sink every shot you take, but the more you take, the more chances you have to succeed. Conversely, if you do not take your shots, you never have a chance.

> **"I've missed more than 9,000 shots in my career.**
> **I've lost almost 300 games. 26 times, I've been trusted to**
> **take the game winning shot and missed. I've failed over**
> **and over and over again in my life.**
> **And that is why I succeeded."**
> **— *MICHAEL JORDAN***

To continue the basketball metaphor, when you shoot, you at least will know if the ball goes in or whether you miss. Even if you do miss, you have some idea of why—that is, perhaps you shot the ball too hard, too soft, too far left, or too far right. You learn from your previous mistake and then you adapt your strategy for the next shot. And the more shots you take, the better you will be.

Isn't this how we become great at anything? Sports, life, leadership, career, relationships? Skills are never developed overnight. They are developed over time through practice, practice, and even more practice.

> **"You always miss 100 percent of the shots you never take."**
> **— *WAYNE GRETZKY***

The Wayne Gretzky quote is as true in life as it is in hockey. No one is perfect. We all take bad shots from time to time. We all make mistakes and, sometimes, things just don't work out the way we hoped. Failure is an unavoidable part of the human experience. What scares most people is the irony of the situation—the fact that the more you try, the more chance for failure you will have.

But the reverse is true as well. Each effort you make also prepares and provides another opportunity for success.

It is critical to understand and apply the fact that failure and mistakes are also a source of wisdom. When we have the right attitude, we can learn from our errors. And each error we learn from makes us more unstoppable the next time.

The world's most successful people are those who recognize and accept that failure is part of the success process! In my opinion, this—more than anything—is what we should be teaching our youth. Take risk. Try. Learn. Try again. Fail forward. Succeed.

"A failure is not always a mistake.
The real mistake is to stop trying."
— B. F. SKINNER

Why are these concepts so difficult to apply in our daily lives? Why do so many of us quit so often or get frustrated when things don't go our way? We expect life to be easy, and when it's not, we beat ourselves up. We're much too hard on ourselves.

One of the secrets of learning from failure is to ask yourself positive questions to get the results you want. For instance, when things don't go your way, don't berate yourself with statements like, *"I can't believe I made such a huge*

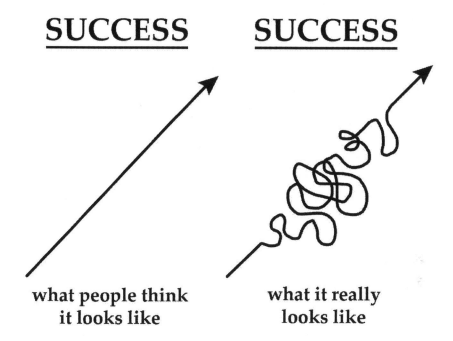

SUCCESS   SUCCESS

what people think   **what it really**
it looks like   **looks like**

mistake!" or "I'm an idiot!" Instead ask yourself, *"What can I learn from this experience?"* and *"How does this experience make me better?"*

When you're stopped short of your goal or when something difficult happens to you or gets in your way, instead of asking why these things always happen to you, ask yourself how you can learn from this situation so that it never happens again.

This mindset is difficult at first but when you learn to apply this approach for dealing with obstacles, the world and every experience you desire is at your fingertips. You can never lose if you never give up. You can always learn something, even when you don't get your desired result, but this only happens when you ask yourself the right questions.

Have you heard the saying "garbage in; garbage out?"

The same applies here. Ask yourself a bad question, and you will get a bad answer. Ask yourself a positive question, and you will get a positive answer.

Happiness and fulfillment are determined by focus.

SUCCESS

Rejection equals redirection.

Struggles develop strengths.

Setbacks are setups.

Mistakes are teachable moments.

Hard work always beats talent when talent doesn't work hard.

SUCCESS

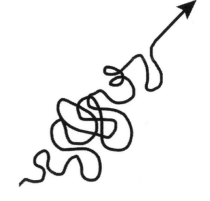

what it really looks like

What you think about, you bring about. We're all a work in progress, like wet clay, and being influential for others is as simple as understanding and applying this positive philosophy and approach to life.

Again, you can never lose when you ask yourself the right questions. Help someone else learn this philosophy today, because we all are educators in some way. When you hear someone say something negative about themselves or their situation, ask them, *"What did this experience teach you?"* or *"How did this make you better?"* You'll be amazed at their positive reaction when you empower them to reflect on the lesson learned.

When I worked in Student Affairs as a Dean of Students, I applied this concept with our students. In my office when students talked negatively about themselves or when I was talking with them about a tense judicial situation, I would always ask, *"So, what is the teachable moment here? How does this experience make you better?"* And my favorite, *"So, if you were to go back in time, what would you do differently?"*

Their answers would often lead us to discuss topics that ran even deeper than the reason for which they'd come into my office. Sometimes there would be tears and high emotions, and if appropriate, I would suggest they talk to one of our counselors down the hall. I was thrilled when a student agreed because it meant the student was willing to deal with the root issue and might be ready to reprogram their mind in a positive-thinking direction. To me, that's personal development!

Back to you ... whether it's a bad experience at your job, the end of a relationship, disappointing feedback you just received, a rejection of some sort—whatever. It doesn't matter. It was a bad experience and possibly a situation with a major setback.

But if you immediately ask yourself the right questions, then despite the bad experience, you are still taking a step toward being a better person. Possibly, you're being pushed out of your own nest. That door may have closed, but a beautiful window of new opportunity has just opened!

> "A great many years ago I purchased a fine dictionary.
> The first thing I did with it was to turn to the word
> 'impossible' and neatly cut it out of the book."
> — *NAPOLEON HILL*, THINK AND GROW RICH

In this chapter, we've reviewed several famous and amazing people: Roger Bannister, Jack Canfield, Mark Victor Hansen, and Michael Jordan.

What do all these people have in common?

They all *thought differently*. Their success was a direct result of their conditioned mindset that understood the real meaning of "NO" as "New Opportunity." They had a clear vision of their goals and consistently asked themselves positive questions, even when they experienced obstacles, frustrations and naysayers. Where others might have quit, these individuals persisted because they believed in themselves and learned from each of their failures. Their failures made them better, and they faced each new opportunity with the lessons their previous failures had taught them. And today, we remember them for their achievements and honor them for their persistence.

Watch "A Motivational Video" by visiting
http://kevincsnyder.com/free-stuff

• *BEFORE YOU GO* •

Before moving on to the next chapter, take a moment to reflect on how you feel right now so you can return to review your thoughts at a later date.

What did you learn from this chapter?

_____

_____

_____

_____

What surprised you?

_____

_____

_____

_____

What affirmed what you already know?

_____

_____

_____

_____

What are you now ready for?

_____

_____

_____

_____

What is something new you desire in your life?

_____

_____

_____

_____

I Lived My Dream

"There are two types of dreams. The ones we have when we're sleeping and the ones we make when we're awake."
— *KEVIN C. SNYDER*

G rowing up, I was obsessed with *The Price Is Right* game show hosted by Bob Barker. The show captivated me in ways I still do not understand.

My mom and I watched the show every single day while having lunch. We'd vicariously play along with the show and find ourselves screaming at the television when one of the contestants made a silly bid. During the Showcase Showdown, Mom and I would bet against each other and compete to see who was closest to the actual retail price of the showdown package. The loser had to clean up lunch!

When we were shopping at the grocery store, Mom and I practiced price-checking items. She'd quiz me on anything she felt might be a product on *The Price is Right*.

"Macaroni & cheese?" she'd ask me.

"$1.99!" I'd reply.

"Prune juice?" she'd ask again.

"$5.99!" I'd answer.

And my favorite ...

"Metamucil?"

"$9.49!"

What 12-year-old kid knows the price of products like prune juice and Metamucil?

"Repetition is the mother of skill." — *TONY ROBBINS*

So, if you want to be good at something, you practice. If you want to be great, practice even more.

In college, the days before there was On Demand television, DVRs and electronic equipment where you could record what you wanted and watch it whenever you wanted, I deliberately scheduled my classes around *The Price is Right*. I never scheduled a college course at that magical hour of eleven a.m. just so I could watch Bob Barker host the show every single day!

During my freshman year of college, I even wrote an English paper on the show and received a grade of "See me after class" from the instructor, Dr. Lavonne Adams. When I nervously visited her office after class, I thought I was in trouble. I expected her to tell me it was the worst paper she had ever read. I prepared myself to hear her advise me that I needed help in writing.

When I arrived at her office, Dr. Adams asked me to sit down. She then held up a copy of my paper and said, "Kevin, in all my years of teaching, this is one of the best papers I've ever read." She paused and smiled.

Then she continued, "But you're obsessed with this show, aren't you? I can tell you are very good at it! Well, just so you know, I'm a *Price is Right* fanatic myself! I thoroughly enjoyed reading your paper and with your permission, I'd like to share it with our English faculty. Is that OK?"

I was shocked. I sat there in disbelief. I walked away from her office thinking to myself, "Maybe I'm not so dumb after all." You see, when Dr. Adams told me I was really good at writing, I started believing it too. And because I believed I was good at writing, I started writing more. I started writing even better. I started writing with more confidence, and I looked forward to writing rather than fearing and dreading it.

Isn't it amazing how one person can impact your belief system about yourself with one comment? The power of our words is extraordinary.

You don't know my teenage struggles quite yet, but you'll read more about them in the following chapters.

Despite growing up in a loving family with two amazing parents, I battled self-esteem issues.

My high school grades were mediocre at best, and I had to work hard to even make "C's." Barely making it through high school, I applied to just one college because that's the only college where I thought I had a chance at being accepted.

I still remember receiving my SAT (standardized test for college admission) score of 870 as a high school senior. Most of my friends had made 1100+ on their scores, which was always difficult for me to hear. I was jealous. They seemed effortlessly smarter than I was, had clearer goals than I did and displayed much more confidence in themselves than I ever could. If they only knew how much mental baggage I was invisibly carrying.

The day I received my SAT score in the mail, I cried. I felt like a fool. I ripped up the score report and quickly burned it in the fireplace. For weeks, I told my Mom I had never received it. I knew it was a matter of time before she would simply order a replacement score report. And she did.

I saw the duplicate copy of the score report in the mail. But I didn't open it. I waited for Mom to get home, and I handed it to her with a tear in my eye.

I don't remember our conversation, but I remember saying to her, "I'm sorry I'm so stupid, Mom. I did the best I could."

I just remember her holding me.

❖

I'm sure it was by a very thin thread, but I was accepted into the only college where I applied, the University of North Carolina at Wilmington. I knew I wanted to major in Marine Biology. I also knew I would struggle in every class. So therefore, every time I had math homework, I would visit the math tutor lab immediately after class and get help. Every time I had a writing assignment, I would visit the Writing Center and get help. Every time a faculty instructor held an exam review session, I attended and sat in the front row.

I was aware I wasn't the sharpest tool in the shed, or so I said to myself, but that didn't stop me from giving it my all. It was up to me and no one else. The more I attended tutor labs and exam review sessions, the better I understood the material. I was also shocked at how few other students took advantage of these free resources.

I'll never forget one review session where the chemistry instructor, Dr. James Boyle, gave us the exact answers to the exam in advance. Our class had more than 300 students and only four of us showed up for the review session. I was just as surprised as Dr. Boyle was frustrated. Dr. Boyle said to us, "Ninety percent of your success in life is going to result from you showing up when others do not. Those who show up are rewarded." He then handed us the actual test and discussed each answer. I made a 100—a perfect score—on that test not because I was the smartest tool in the shed, but because I showed up.

All I wanted in high school was to be normal. In college though, I discovered that nothing was normal. Everything was unique. Different. "Normal" was a ghost and I was chasing it.

My first-year roommate, Duncan, was brilliant academically. I heard him bragging one day about making a 1530 on the SAT—a near perfect score. I was envious of him. I wanted to be like him. However, because Duncan thought he could rely on his intellect instead of work ethic, he chose not to attend classes. He did show up for college parties though, and he seemed to show up well with the ladies who visited our dorm room.

It took only a semester for Duncan to flunk out of college. I assumed he would make straight "A's" in his classes despite never attending them. Nope. He earned straight "F's." I remember the day his mom showed up unexpectedly to our dorm room and started packing his bags while he was sleeping and hung over from a prior late-night party.

On the other hand, my first semester in college I made straight "A's"—a perfect 4.0 GPA. But not because of my intellect. My academic achievement was a direct result from my work ethic. A quote my dad shared with me long ago rings true to this:

> "Hard work beats talent when talent doesn't work hard." — *JACK SNYDER*

Although the beginning of my first year of college was extremely challenging, it was transformational for me in so many different ways. That time was a new beginning for me, a genesis, to begin planting new seeds in the fertile soil of my mind. These seeds would ultimately grow into a *think differently* mindset that would change my entire life. After the first semester, I discovered I could not only survive, but I would thrive—and excel.

From chemistry professor Dr. Boyle, I learned about the power of showing up and being present for an opportunity. From English professor Dr. Adams, I learned about the power of following your passion and being better at it the more you do it. Several other teachers and administrators made a difference in my life during my first year of college when I never really expected to make it through.

Because of the support and encouragement I received, despite being a struggling, disconnected first-year student, I would eventually realize that I wanted to help other students like me by working in Student Affairs. I wanted to be the teacher who could help other students who were struggling like me. I wanted to be the Director of Student Activities who would help other disengaged students like me. I wanted to be the Dean of Students to identify and advocate for students like me.

I learned so much about myself that first year in so many ways. I received letters from the Deans of the English department, the Chemistry department, and the Math department informing me that my instructors had noticed my interest and discipline in the subject material. In each letter, they commended me and asked me to consider changing my intended major to English, Chemistry, or Math, respectively. Instead of ripping up these letters as I did my SAT score, I framed them. And because these esteemed individuals— strangers really—saw something in me, I started seeing it too. Although I had no clue what "it" was.

Now that you have a bit more background about my

struggles growing up, back to my *Price is Right* story in college ...

After my conversation with Dr. Adams, I continued arranging my college class schedule around *The Price is Right* and never missed an episode. Then it happened ...

During my junior year of college, I attended a student leadership conference. I'll be honest, I didn't want to be there, but I "showed up" anyway.

In the registration line, I met Chris, an eccentric guy with a funny personality. We became instant friends. During one of the conference breakout sessions, we participated in an icebreaker where we had to stand on top of a chair and share something unique about ourselves. When it was his turn, Chris stood on his chair and announced he had just returned from a spring break trip where he appeared on *The Price Is Right* and won a gazebo!

Amazed and envious, I nearly fell off my chair! Chris had no prior knowledge of my obsession with the show. Meeting him felt to me like a divine sign, and I knew I was destined to be on *The Price Is Right* as well. Before this, I had never met anyone who had been on the show. Meeting Chris was the example, the nudge and the catalyst that I needed to push myself to actually get on the show like he did.

At that specific moment, I made the conscious decision that I too would someday be on *The Price Is Right* and shake hands with Bob Barker on stage. I truly believed and mentally envisioned I would not only be a contestant but also a winner.

Even though I had no idea how to get on the show, there was no doubt in my mind that this dream would come true.

**"When you decide it in your mind,
it becomes only a matter of time."**
— *KEVIN C. SNYDER*

Throughout that leadership conference, I questioned Chris about his experience and absorbed the advice he shared about being selected as a contestant. He explained to me that there was a *strategy* for being selected as a contestant on the show. Chris told me that prior to the show starting, the producers know exactly who will be chosen. He suggested taking advantage of the time standing in line while waiting to enter the studio. "The secret," he said, "is that the producers scan for contestants before the show even starts—that is how they select 'Contestants Row.'"

I learned that potential contestants who stand out or are in large, exuberant groups of people have a better chance of hearing those magical words, "Come on down!"

After learning all this, the "how" of my dream became crystal clear. I was convinced that if I traveled from my home in Durham, North Carolina, to Burbank, California, and could somehow become part of a noticeable group, the producers would see the excitement in my eyes, and my dream of shaking Bob Barker's hand on *The Price is Right* would manifest.

Since Chris lived in California, he agreed to be the

ringleader who would organize my tribe. We kept in touch, hoping to find an available date where I could drive across the country and enact the plan. A few months prior to my college graduation, I ordered tickets for the show.

Unfortunately, the only show taping date we could coordinate for our adventure was the same date as my own college graduation!

As difficult as the decision was, I knew that pursuing my dream of being on *The Price is Right* would be incredibly fulfilling and exciting. Driving across the country and sacrificing my college graduation seemed to make my pursuit even *more* worthwhile. Besides, doesn't everything have a sacrifice component to it?

> **"There are always reasons not to do something.
> What we have to focus on are the reasons
> why we should." — KEVIN C. SNYDER**

I decided to go, which meant I skipped my college graduation. While my classmates were preparing to graduate, I was driving to meet and live my destiny.

Three long days and 3,000 miles after leaving North Carolina, I finally arrived in Los Angeles and connected with Chris and his friends. Chris had corralled more than 20 people to go with us and help me get noticed to be selected for the show.

The next morning our car caravan headed out toward *The Price is Right* studio parking lot in Burbank. I was so excited, I could hardly contain myself.

As we pulled into the parking lot, I was reminded of a movie scene from *National Lampoon's Vacation*—the one where the Griswalds travel to Wally World only to discover that the amusement park was closed!

We had a similar situation. When we pulled into the parking lot, *The Price is Right* parking lot was *E-M-P-T-Y!* The sign on the parking lot fence read:

Today's show is CANCELLED

In disbelief, I stumbled from the car and sat on the asphalt. I felt sick to my stomach.

A security guard soon appeared and informed us that Bob Barker was sick, and they had cancelled the show for the remainder of the week. He also asked us to leave the property. In front of everyone, I screamed, and tears flooded down my face. My graduation ceremony had been sacrificed for nothing. My entire trip was worthless.

I had no choice but to start driving back home the next day. During the drive, all sorts of crazy thoughts were going through my mind. Every emotion you can imagine came and went, including all the negative head trash from my teenage years. At times I would scream out loud at the long highway in front of me.

I'll never forget being in Tennessee, though, nearly home to North Carolina and suddenly hearing a voice. Yes, a voice. It was more than my mind asking itself a question. I literally heard a voice inside my head so loud that I thought someone was speaking to me. I clearly remember driving on Interstate 40 near Knoxville, Tennessee, when this voice asked me a question:

"How bad do I want it?" I repeated out loud, looking around. Where had that voice, that question, come from? It was a surreal moment. Nothing like this had ever happened to me before. It was either a spiritual situation or food poisoning from the Cracker Barrel where I had just eaten!

Although the voice scared me at first, I quickly realized it was only my mind asking itself a question—somewhat intensely! Sitting in that car I had quite a bit of time to think, reflect, and be mindful. The power of my thoughts spoke to me quite loudly. I began to think about my answer. "How bad *do* I want it? How bad *do* I want it?"

What was my answer to my own voice?

I wanted it BAD! In fact, more than anything else I had ever wanted in my life. *The Price Is Right* was my first dream. It seemed silly to others, but it was *my* dream and that's all that mattered. I had never had a dream before that seemed so clear in my mind. Being on the show and shaking hands with Bob Barker on stage was a vision I expected to manifest and come true.

Despite my disappointment and shock from the show being cancelled that week, my dream of someday being a contestant on *The Price Is Right* was only strengthened through this first failed attempt.

When I returned home, I received lots of phone calls from friends who had heard about what happened. They couldn't believe it either. I also kept in touch with Chris, knowing I would need his help again.

I didn't realize it at the time, but I was beginning to understand and teach myself that the most important things in life require belief, dedication, and sacrifice.

Six months later, I called Chris to tell him that I was ready to try again. After picking our date and ordering tickets for the show, I purchased a plane ticket to Los Angeles. Chris was in charge of arranging another energetic caravan of supporters to go with us.

I arrived to the airport at 11 p.m., and Chris and his friends were waiting to take me straight to CBS television studios. We arrived to the parking lot at 2 a.m. and once again it was EMPTY! However, this time was different. The parking lot was empty because we were first in line!

Nearly eight hours later at 10 a.m., with more than 1,000 other eager contestants behind us, I noticed staff walking through the lines. This was it! My moment to convince them to select me for *Contestants' Row* had arrived.

When the producers reached our group, one of them asked me, "Where are you all from?"

I inhaled and quickly managed to babble the twenty seconds version of my *Price is Right* obsession and tell them about my life-long devotion to the show. Today, years later, I don't really remember what I said. I do recall the producers laughing and their eyes growing to a size of golf balls, but they gave no indication they would be calling my name on the show.

As they moved onward to the other thousand people waiting in line, Chris rolled his eyes and said, "Dude, you are crazy-train for this show! I hope they do select you so you can move on with your life!"

All I could do now was try to control the butterflies in my stomach and wait. I hated waiting. A few hours later, we were finally led into the television studio. I could barely sit still as I waited for the show to start. When *The Price is Right* theme music started, I literally closed my eyes and prayed to hear my own name called out, along with an invitation to "come on down!" to *Contestants' Row*.

Contestant Number One was called. **Not me.**

Contestant Number Two was called. **Not me.**

Contestant Number Three was called,
and I heard those magical words ...

"KEVIN SNYDER, COME ON DOWN! YOU'RE THE NEXT CONTESTANT ON *THE PRICE IS RIGHT*!"

To watch my "Price is Right" video where I get called down to Contestants' Row, *visit* http://kevincsnyder.com/free-stuff *(1 min)*

Wwwhhhooooaaaaahhhhhh!! That moment was a complete blur, but it's all on video— me wildly jumping up and down, knocking Chris to the floor. It's both hilarious and humbling to watch. Just visit my website to view the video yourself or type in *"Kevin Snyder meets Bob Barker"* on Youtube.com.

Kevin meets his hero, Bob Barker.

My date with destiny and Bob Barker had finally arrived. I was on *Contestants' Row*. And because I had studied the show and knew how to play every game, I was more than confident I would soon be on stage shaking hands and living my dream with Bob Barker.

I did not win the first prize on *Contestant's Row*—I underbid. However, on the second item, I placed a near perfect bid on a diamond bracelet—and WON! After toppling Chris over yet again in excitement, I ran onstage to Bob, shook his hand, placed my hand on my chest and relished the surreal moment of my dream coming true live on television.

I do not remember what happened next so, again, I'm relieved there is video that witnessed the account.

Onstage, I played "Punch-a-Bunch," a game where I could win prizes and up to $10,000 in cash. I ended up winning all the prizes, resulting in four punches on the money board. Each punch hole contained a specific amount of money. From one of my punches Bob pulled out $5,000! I won BIG—or at least big for a kid just out of college!

My total prize winnings were the diamond bracelet, a steam vacuum, a napkin holder, a wicker basket, a milkshake maker, and the $5,000!

(*Note: Neither the steam vacuum nor the milkshake maker ever worked!*)

After celebrating that night with Chris, I reflected on this journey of literally living my dream.

Though some may call my dream crazy or even silly, my *Price Is Right* journey is a true story demonstrating how living a dream is possible. I'm living proof.

Being on this show changed my life, and it has continued to impact my life every day since. I wouldn't be where I am without having gone through the experience. This experience is also a signature story in my keynote presentations, and it's always the energetic highlight with my audiences. The story is what connects me with people the most. As for me, every time I share the story, it feels as if it's happening for the first time.

The lesson of this story is not that I finally made it on my favorite game show or that I won money and prizes. The journey I have shared in this chapter is about taking time to identify and live your dream. Your dream is waiting for you. It's waiting for you even if you haven't identified it or if it's been dormant in your mind for the past few years.

Let this chapter be a testimony for you. Allow my story to be a catalyst in your own life that empowers you to take life to a new level. It's time for you to live your dream because no one can do it for you.

WHAT IS YOUR the PRICE is Right ?

Take a moment to reflect on your desires and ask yourself what your passions are in life, no matter what they are or how silly they may seem. Don't think one second about what anyone else will think. Don't make assumptions you can't accomplish it or that you're not good enough. Don't convince yourself life is too busy or that your family situation just won't allow it right now. If you have children, know that the best way to inspire them is to show them by example!

So, what is it you want? What makes you come alive? Because those desires have been placed there for a reason!

What desire(s) is in your heart that you cannot explain?

_____
_____
_____
_____
_____
_____

What makes you come alive when thinking about it?

_____

_____

_____

_____

_____

_____

Your desire is as unique for you as your fingerprint. Once you identify what it is you desire and *will* accomplish, you must persistently take action to manifest it in your life. Don't you want to inspire others around you by your example?

SO HOW BAD DO **YOU** *WANT IT?*

Even though you may—like me and everyone else—fail at times during the pursuit, recognize that failure and setbacks can teach and inspire us the most. If it's a healthy desire, we want it even more, and we know it's just a matter of time before we achieve it.

Even when an experience is negative, frustrating, and appears to be an insurmountable obstacle, realize that in facing it, in accepting and learning from it, you are better for having experienced it. It is there to both *teach* and *test* you. Your perseverance alone is a testimony that will inspire others. Your commitment to your own vision and expectation will change other people's lives.

I'm incredibly honored and humbled to share my *Price is Right* experience with hundreds of thousands of people all over the world. Just like your story can, will, and probably even already has, my story has inspired thousands of people in ways I never expected. Until I *lived* my dream, to everyone but me it was just a silly dream.

> *I am Roger Bannister—in my own way.*
> *I am Jack Canfield and Mark Victor Hansen—*
> *in my own way.*
> *I am Michael Jordan—in my own way.*
>
> *And so are YOU!*

Whenever I feel overwhelmed or frustrated, I only need to recall those magical words, *"Kevin Snyder, come on down!"* and I know all my dreams are attainable. All I need is persistence and faith.

And every time I share my *Price is Right* story in a presentation, I continue to live a new dream of professional speaking in real time, because our passions are cyclical (as you'll read in the next chapter). When pursuing our passions, doors will open that we don't even see at the time.

My *Price is Right* story has one universal message to which we all can relate:

"You can't live a dream until you have one first."
— KEVIN C. SNYDER

So, what is your Price is Right? What is your dream?

What are you waiting on?

"The time is always right to do what is right.
Never stop dreaming."
— *MARTIN LUTHER KING, JR.*

I'll close this chapter in true Bob Barker fashion:

"Help control the pet population.
Remember to have your pets spayed and neutered.
Goodbye, everybody!"
— *BOB BARKER*

• *BEFORE YOU GO* •

Before moving on to the next chapter, take a moment to reflect on how you feel right now so you can return to review your thoughts at a later date.

What did you learn from this chapter?

_____

_____

_____

_____

What surprised you?

_____

_____

_____

_____

What affirmed what you already know?

_____

_____

_____

_____

What are you now ready for?

_____

_____

_____

_____

What is something new you desire in your life?

_____

_____

_____

_____

PASSION

"When you have passion for something,
you will find a way to make it happen."
— *ZIG ZIGLAR*

I believe one simple word embodies *the key for living a fulfilled life*. It's the source of happiness, living an authentic life, and finding purpose in what we do.

The word is ***PASSION***.

If we are not passionate about what we do, we won't aspire to reach our full potential nor will we enjoy the process in trying to reach it. Passion must be the root, the foundation, of our pursuits. If you don't love what you're doing, not only will it show but, more importantly, you won't be happy. And if you're not happy doing something, then why do it?

Most of us know how to identify and set worthwhile goals. But have you ever set a goal that eventually became less and less interesting over a period of a few weeks or months? Or were you perhaps initially motivated but after a while, your motivation fizzled away?

Unlike motivation, passion is a fuel that never runs dry. Passionate pursuit of a goal will never feel cumbersome or be a chore; rather, it will continue to be an exciting and enjoyable experience. The more you pursue your passion, the more excited and fulfilled you become.

> "All achievement must begin with an intense,
> burning desire and passion for something definite."
> — *NAPOLEON HILL*, THINK AND GROW RICH

Goals we are passionate about are simply glorious to pursue. Yet sometimes we still hesitate to invest our time, talent, and energies toward these passionate pursuits. Why?

Think about it. How many hours of the day do you spend doing something you honestly love, something you are passionate about?

Respectfully, if you are like most people, you spend the majority of your day doing things you "have to do." You will spend very little time, if any at all, on those things that truly inspire you and make time stop.

Some of you might already be thinking, "I am passionate about my family, Kevin."

Yes, you are! And I am honored you have reflected on my question! So, let's take a step back and make a caveat that loved ones—that is, children and/or family—are one exception to my question. I know, not fair.

Still—although your family is likely your number one priority, and rightly so—for just a moment, let's focus only on you and your dreams and aspirations beyond family. What makes time stop outside of family time? If you had a day all to yourself and could do anything, what would you like to do? How many hours of the week do you spend on something you are truly passionate about, something just for you?

> *Where do you spend most of your time?*
> *Doing things you feel you "have to do" OR*
> *things you are "passionate about doing"?*

Try this out. If you kept a journal for one week, or even one day, you could easily identify where you invest most of your time. Moreover, you might be shocked at how much of your day or week is spent being busy with things you feel you "have to do." More importantly, you might identify how little time you invest in yourself and the things you truly are interested in and that make you come alive.

Unfortunately, most people never challenge themselves with these questions. Most of us are so busy with things we convince ourselves we "have to do" that we may never make time to pursue what makes us come alive.

Have you ever watched a hamster or a gerbil spinning a wheel in its cage? The hamster is moving that wheel, but where is it actually going?

That hamster is going absolutely *nowhere*.

We all feel like a hamster at times. It is natural to become so busy we lose sight of what is most important in our lives. In fact, there might be days and weeks when we feel we have no choice regarding how we spend our time. But it's during these moments and days when we must say "no" to accepting additional mundane tasks or allowing those tasks to consume us. It is during these times when we must *refuse to relinquish control* over own lives. We must say "yes" to taking time each day, or at least each week, for ourselves.

Do not give control of your life to something less important than yourself and what you believe in. Is your busy schedule truly more important than your health and well-being, your family, and your success?

Here's one way to find more passion on a daily basis. It's a tip I use every day.

> *Choose something each and every day*
> *to look forward to.*

Even though there are times I may have to work at finding something, I still manage to look forward to something every day. Try it. I did, and it changed my life.

WHAT WILL YOU LOOK FORWARD TO TODAY?

If today is nearly passed, then how about tomorrow? Write it down!

_____

_____

_____

_____

_____

_____

_____

_____

Once you identify something—anything—for each day, make a list and post it somewhere where you will see it. For example, place it in your car, your bathroom, on your refrigerator, or over your office computer. Heck, make copies and place them everywhere! Surround yourself with these reminders of what will make you happy. You will feel transformed and your days will be more enjoyable because, no matter what happens, you have something to look forward to.

You will have to schedule time to enjoy some of your "look forwards," but when you do, know that it is *your time* and no one else's. Honor that time for yourself. You deserve it, and it'll show in other areas of your life as well. Even the busiest people have 15-30 minutes each day to spend on themselves. It's just a matter of the choices we make. Every single person on our planet has the exact same amount of time each day. The difference is in how we invest it.

Life is mainly about your choices. So, what will you choose? Will you simply "be busy" all the time, or will you choose something to look forward to each day? By choosing the second option, I am confident you will immediately feel more fulfilled and passionate!

> *Each day, spend 15-30 minutes on something you are interested in and passionate about.*

People frequently ask me how they can find their passion. This question is one of the reasons I decided to write this book. Yet, it is a question I can only partially answer. My answer is not your answer, and your answer is not someone else's answer. Your passions and interests are unique to you, just as mine are to me. I can only provide concepts to help you discover them.

However, when asked this question, I respond by asking a person what they enjoy spending time on. Quite often, I find they don't know how to invest time in themselves. These are the "busy people" I have referred to. They have not taken control of their life—rather, their life has taken control of them.

Taking time for yourself each day is not selfish. You might say you have far too many responsibilities right now or your finances won't allow you to do anything but work. Perhaps you're in a relationship that makes it difficult to block out free time or you take care of someone who literally takes up all hours of the day. Some of the most common reasons I hear are:

- *I don't have time.*
- *I don't have enough money.*
- *I have kids and a family who need my attention.*
- *I'm overweight.*
- *I'm not strong enough.*
- *I'm too old.*
- *I'm too young.*

With sincere respect to your circumstances, what you've actually done is manifest a list of reasons that, in a circular fashion, will justify what you tend to believe about your situation. If you believe you are "far too busy" to pursue what excites you, then you inevitably will *become* just that—far too busy. The right question isn't, Do I *have* time? Rather, it should be, How can I *make* time to do what I enjoy? Similarly, leaning on any other "excuse" will only reinforce your negative thoughts on why you can't live your passion. Remember, what you think about, you bring about.

What are the reasons *you* typically make for why you cannot pursue something just for you?

> **"Whether you think you can or cannot, you're exactly right."— HENRY FORD**

What you focus on attracts more of the same into your life. When you tell yourself you can or cannot do something, you will attract more of that reality like a magnet.

Here's another way of looking at it. Your life is consistently made up of the orders you give it. For example, when you place an order in a restaurant, what do you expect your server to deliver to your table? You expect them to bring you exactly what you ordered, yes? If they brought you a different meal, wouldn't you send it back?

We give mental orders to ourselves hundreds of times each day. We tell ourselves we can or cannot do something, thus "placing an order" with our life's guiding force. Tell yourself you don't have time and, surprise, you won't have time because *that's* what you ordered. Tell yourself you don't have enough money and, surprise, you won't. You ordered those circumstances yourself, and the universe is delivering as ordered plus fries. Tell yourself you are too young or too old, and you will be exactly right. Whatever you receive—whether positive or negative—will be exactly correct because *you ordered it.*

It's time to get rid of reasons *why you shouldn't* and focus on reasons *why you should.* Invest your mental energy on reasons why you *can* do something rather than why you *cannot.* This is what I am asking you to do: Change your thinking so your life can change.

Unfortunately, most people spend more time and attention on identifying excuses rather than on finding creative ways to accomplish what they desire. They order excuses, and that's what is delivered to their life's dinner table.

Applying this philosophy will require work at first, especially if it is a new concept for you. The idea of "manifesting" a better life, to create an opportunity to pursue your passions and interests, to have more time, more money— whatever your dreams may be—may at first sound like so much voodoo. But as you make this mindset a habitual routine in daily situations, you'll soon discover it is one hundred percent real and valid. This mindset works. I'm living proof and so are countless others.

By placing a "positive order" with your psyche, you will take control of your own life and become the true master of your focus. You will begin to see things in a more positive light which will, in turn, attract more positive things to you. You will be a shining light in the darkness. You will be a positive influence to others. People want to follow someone who is positive and inspired. Embracing and utilizing this approach and philosophy is a personal power most will never even understand. Don't be one of those people.

I believe the secret key to unlock and unleash our potential is to understand our passion and incorporate it in our life. You can lead a more fulfilled, passionate life starting right now—*if* you decide to. Reading the rest of this book won't matter much for you unless you truly have a desire to make a change and take control.

"The reason most people settle for mediocrity is that they have never chosen to master something they truly love."
— *TONY ROBBINS*

I acknowledge that we all have different circumstances, and some of us have responsibilities that might limit how much risk we can take when making a personal life change. Those circumstances and responsibilities do not mean we can make no change at all; rather, it just means we must consider our changes carefully as we move forward. What matters is the effort and action of simply beginning.

From now on, instead of saying to yourself, "No, I have too much responsibility," place yourself in a positive context and ask yourself, "*How* can I manage my responsibilities to still make time for myself?"

You should spend 15-30 minutes each day on something you are interested in and passionate about. What can you look forward to today?

When you ask yourself *how* you can do something, it opens your mind to creatively find the answers.

To watch an inspirational clip titled, "How Bad Do You Want It?" by Erik Thomas, the Hip Hop Preacher, visit http://kevincsnyder.com/free-stuff (6 min)

• *Before You Go* •

Before moving on to the next chapter, take a moment to reflect on how you feel right now so you can return to review your thoughts at a later date.

What did you learn from this chapter?

_____

_____

_____

_____

What surprised you?

_____

_____

_____

_____

What affirmed what you already know?

_____

_____

_____

_____

What are you now ready for?

_____

_____

_____

_____

What is something new you desire in your life?

_____

_____

_____

_____

Lessons
of Wisdom

"Our greatest mistakes can be our greatest lessons learned no other way." — *J.K. ROWLING*

To watch J.K. Rowling's inspirational graduation speech where she talks about the importance of her failures, visit http://kevincsnyder.com/free-stuff (20 min)

We all make mistakes—no one is perfect. In fact, acknowledging and learning from our mistakes builds moral character, fosters integrity, and teaches incredible life lessons.

It's when we choose *not* to learn from our mistakes that we miss the real lesson that life is offering to teach us.

"When you lose, don't lose the lesson."
— *THE DALAI LAMA*

When I was a high school senior, I became president of a show choir organization called *Knightsounds*. Each year, our group traveled to Disney World in Orlando, Florida, to compete in a national singing competition.

My mom was a math teacher at my high school, and she was a chaperone on this one specific trip.

During the tournament that particular year, I became fond of a special girl in the organization. We spent most our free time together in the same group of friends.

While walking around the shops at Disney on the first day, I immediately noticed that this group was shop-lifting at nearly every store we visited—and none of them ever got caught. What disappointed me even more was that the girl I liked was also the main influencer.

After the first day, I decided to simply keep my mouth shut and not say a word to anyone. I certainly did not want to get the group I was with, especially the girl I liked, in trouble. I also did not want to say anything to the group, concerned they would "unwelcome" me from hanging around with them—and her.

At the end of the third and final day of the competition, we were given several hours of free time before we needed to be back on the bus for departure. Of course, I spent this time with the girl I liked and her group of friends.

While in the final shop before heading back toward the bus, I bought a Disney t-shirt. I then waited outside for several minutes. When I returned inside the store to find out what was taking the group so long, I found them shop-lifting again.

This time though, I became tempted to impress and show them I was just as clever as they were. I wanted to fit in and be cool like them. Without even thinking, I looked around, grabbed a Goofy hat and put the hat inside the bag that held the shirt I had purchased.

I looked around again to make sure no one noticed—except, of course, the girl I liked—and then started to walk out of the store. The second I put one foot outside, a hand grabbed my arm and stopped me. Next thing I saw was a police badge and a tall man who said, "Come with me."

My heart skipped a beat, and my legs became immediately numb.

The officer led me to the Disney security station where all my personal information was taken, and I was fingerprinted.

During my final fingerprint, my mom walked in the security room. I had already been crying, but when I saw the shock and disappointment in her eyes, I started bawling.

The music director was also with my mom, and they introduced themselves to the officer handling my incident. The officer explained to them that I had been caught shoplifting.

My mom was speechless. The music director responded to the officer saying, "Kevin is the last person I would ever expect to do such a thing."

Even though the officer could visibly observe my tearful remorse and regret, he stated he was required to file the incident with authorities.

By this time, the bus had already been waiting for several hours. Because of me, everyone was sitting in the bus becoming more restless and angry with each passing moment. When I finally was released in the custody of my mom, I made the longest walk-of-shame you can imagine. I walked inside that bus feeling embarrassed and humiliated. All fifty-three students had been waiting for hours.

I just kept my head down and sat in the front seat next to my mom, not saying a word.

When we stopped for gas, most everyone exited the bus to stretch. I stayed inside the bus, not wanting to talk with anyone. Just when I thought the bus was empty, a girl named Jenny grabbed my arm and said, "Come outside with me."

Not knowing if my classmates wanted to punch me or just yell, I slowly walked outside, expecting the worst.

I didn't know Jenny well. She told me that everyone knew my shoplifting attempt was out of character and that the others in the group I was with were the ones who should have been caught.

Even though the words she shared felt somewhat reassuring, it did not excuse the fact that I had done what I did.

Jenny invited me to sit next to her when we got back on the bus. Reluctantly I agreed, but as the trip progressed, I was so glad I had accepted her invitation.

We talked the remainder of that 10-hour bus ride home through the night. When our bus pulled into the high school parking lot near 7 a.m. the next morning, I saw the high school principal standing at the school entrance. He wasn't there to greet the bus; he was waiting for me. My dad was right behind him, and neither of them was smiling.

Reality set in. Whatever punishment I was about to receive, I knew I deserved it. The principal immediately took me to his office and asked for an explanation. I shared everything and took full responsibility. The principal suspended me for five days despite graduation being less than one month away.

I don't remember all of the details about being "grounded" at home but it was a laundry list of privileges removed—no phone, television, car, activities after school, and so forth.

I deserved everything that was dealt out to me. I was so embarrassed and ashamed of myself for what I had done. More importantly, I had embarrassed my mom as a chaperone and teacher. I had also embarrassed my family's name, my entire school, my music teacher, and the *Knightsounds* organization.

I learned an incredible life lesson about ethics, accountability, and the importance of considering consequences before acting. I also learned first-hand about what happens when you surround yourself by negative influencers.

Those five days I was suspended from school were tough, and I hated being at home in silence. My parents knew I was beating myself up pretty badly, so they called me several times each day to check up on me. After school, friends would also stop by. During that time, I learned who my *real* friends were.

No one from the shoplifting group, including the girl I *had* liked, ever stopped by. Of course, they ultimately were not responsible for my actions; but, for the first time in my life, I learned a lesson about authentic friendship. You should never lead or follow friends down the wrong path.

Jenny visited me every day. She would eventually become my high school sweetheart. She had seen me at my worst and was willing to look beyond it. She accepted me because she knew I was better than my mistake.

When I returned to school after my five days of suspension, it felt just plain weird. I felt like an alien from planet *Zorkon*. Of course, everyone knew what I had done, including teachers and other students. The school newspaper had run a front-page article about my arrest.

On the first day back, I asked the music director if I could share a few words with the group during our meeting. I had written some remarks expressing my sincere apologies and remorse for my selfish behavior. I also volunteered to remove myself as president of the group.

I still have this written speech in my diary. It was a life-changing moment and the first time I remember ever taking responsibility in a group setting.

After making my speech, no one said a word. I didn't make the speech hoping anyone would respond. I just sat down and stared at paint on the wall, wishing the music director would get practice under way. But the awkward silence in the room continued. No one, including the music director, knew what to do or say.

Finally, a voice from the back of the room spoke up

and, even now, more than 20 years later, I still remember every word she shared:

> *"Kevin, speaking to us took courage. Unlike others*
> *in this same room, you were held accountable*
> *for your actions. However, you have taught us all*
> *to own a mistake and that's what leadership is*
> *about. I motion to keep you as President. "*

The room erupted in applause. I was shocked. I didn't know whether to smile or cry. Consumed by the moment, I did both.

Although not the focus of this chapter, I feel compelled to share that neither the girl I *had* liked—before Jenny, of course—nor the group of shoplifters I was with during that Disney trip ever talked to me again. They ignored me. It's as if they felt the same embarrassment as I did but they didn't have the opportunity to acknowledge it in front of others. Or they didn't care to.

Hopefully, though, they learned the same lesson I did.

Our teachable moments can, and should,
serve as lessons of wisdom for others as well.

Even though my school problems seemed to be over, the legal problems were just beginning. Disney did press charges, and I had to obtain legal representation. I pleaded guilty. What I had done was pretty straight forward.

My lawyer was able to reduce the court charge to a misdemeanor based on my prior clean record. Since I was only 17, my record would not show the arrest. It would be expunged once I turned 18 as long as nothing else was added. Thankfully, the legal consequences of this experience would not be a permanent scar on my life.

The attorney cost was $2,000. Even though I had a great neighborhood lawn business and could pay this amount up front, I wanted to make that $2,000 back somehow so that I would never notice it missing from my bank account. I felt that earning an additional $2,000 through a second job would help me put the experience behind me more quickly.

I began working that summer as a waiter at Pizza Inn Restaurant just down the street. I kept a log during each work shift, documenting every hour worked and each tip made. Every dollar bill was saved on my bedroom desk, piling higher and higher each week. My log showed that I averaged $14.28 per hour, earning over $2,000 within two months. (By the way, this was 1994!)

I was surprised to make that much money so quickly and, frankly, so easily. Not everyone at that restaurant did as well as I did—and I was only temporary. I really enjoyed the job and meeting so many new customers each shift was fun. I had amazing conversations with complete strangers that summer.

Once I finally earned $2,000, I asked my dad to take me and my cash piles of $1s, $5s, $10s and $20s to the bank. I'll always remember the awkward look the teller gave me when I handed her $1,100 in $1s!

After I deposited the money, my dad and I went out

for lunch. We talked about how good it felt that my shoplifting experience had finally reached a stage of closure—I felt able to move on. I remember him asking me, "So what did you learn from this experience?"

As I answered him, it struck me how much I had learned. Lessons of accountability, consequences, reputation, influence, relationships, family, leadership, and so much more.

Also, I talked to him about how much I enjoyed being a waiter. When he asked when I was going to quit, I replied that I wasn't—I actually liked being a waiter so much that I was going to continue working at the restaurant. I enjoyed working with people and helping ensure customers had a great experience at the restaurant too much to leave.

For the first time in my life, I realized how important it was for me to work with, and be surrounded by, *people*. Prior to this experience, the only job I ever had was my lawn business, which was a solitary and monotonous job of walking around in circles. The money was incredible, but there was no true fulfillment or interaction with anyone.

In addition to the lawn business, and instead of serving pizza, I found a new serving job at an upscale restaurant across town. I did very well there, too, but I realized that more than the financial benefits, I looked forward to working each day and meeting new people. It was clear to me that my personality flourished when I worked with and was surrounded by people. That is Lesson #2 learned from my shoplifting experience that I would not have learned otherwise.

Lesson #1, first and foremost, was about

accountability and responsibility. When you make a mistake, own it. Not only must you acknowledge it, but you must also learn from it. Everyone makes mistakes, but to ignore the lesson within them is the real mistake. Allow mistakes to serve as springboards of wisdom so that you can be a *better* person, not a *bitter* person.

"The only mistakes are those we don't learn from."
— *KEVIN C. SNYDER*

The lessons I learned from my shoplifting mistake came to me the hard way. But the important thing is that I *did* learn. I was also fortunate to have fallen into my error at a time in my life when the long-range consequences were minimal. For that I am very grateful.

Lesson #3 was a hidden gem—Jenny's grace and acceptance. We dated for nearly two years after that incident. I would not have met her if it were not for the shoplifting experience. Not only did she appear in my life during an incredibly difficult time, but she was there for me when others were not. She accepted my faults and bad judgments. Her grace taught me my decision was not reflective of who I was. Rather, it was simply a poor decision I learned from.

Looking back on this entire experience, I am amazed and grateful to have learned so much. I am a better person as a result of it, but only because I recognized this mistake as a lesson of wisdom.

Never regret anything that has happened in your life. It's led you to where you are today. It cannot be changed, undone, or forgotten. Take it as a lesson learned and move on. Your scars are beautiful. Bloom where you are planted.

To watch a very special inspirational video titled "The Truth!", visit http://kevincsnyder.com/free-stuff (2 min)

• BEFORE YOU GO •

Before moving on to the next chapter, take a moment to reflect on how you feel right now so you can return to review your thoughts at a later date.

What did you learn from this chapter?

_____

_____

_____

_____

What surprised you?

_____

_____

_____

_____

What affirmed what you already know?

_____

_____

_____

_____

What are you now ready for?

_____

_____

_____

_____

What is something new you desire in your life?

_____

_____

_____

_____

Your Greatest Accomplishment

"The things most important to us
are also the things we have to work hardest for."
— *KEVIN C. SNYDER*

T ake a moment to identify one of your greatest accomplishments—something personal that you are most proud of. What is it?

You might have several experiences or accomplishments that come to mind, but for now, select the one experience most significant and important to you. Now, write about this accomplishment in the space below:

_____

_____

_____

_____

As you recall this accomplishment, reflect on the following two questions:

Was this accomplishment a result of luck?

***Did this accomplishment come easily
and "overnight"?***

These are powerful questions that I have asked hundreds of thousands of people in my speeches. Hearing their answers and knowing my own, I strongly believe that the accomplishment you identified involved sacrifice, hard work, and dedication. I also suspect your greatest accomplishment was a direct result of significant, persistent effort over a long period of time. I would be very surprised if it was the result of something that was easy or that happened overnight.

Am I correct?

If I am not correct, I sincerely would love to hear from you. Please tell me more.

But seriously, think about your most proud accomplishment. Our greatest accomplishments do *not* result from luck. Rather, our proudest experiences result from our *sacrifice* to attain what we most desire and the persistent action we take over time to reach that goal.

**"Ambition is the path to success.
Persistence is the vehicle you arrive in."
— *BILL BRADLEY***

However, what does our fast-paced culture want us to think?

Our societal concepts of *instant coffee* and *instant success* imply that we should not necessarily have to work hard to get our coffee or achieve our dreams and that obstacles should be overcome easily. Society seems to imply that if we encounter obstacles or setbacks, it is because we ourselves are doing something incorrectly. Some of us are afraid of failure—possibly because of our inflated concern for the approval of others. Unfortunately, this fear of failure is sometimes stronger than our desire for success!

However, this fear is debilitating and mistakenly placed. By believing it, we may get caught in the rat race of trying to live a fast-paced, easy, and safe life devoid of failure and obstacles. This is impossible even for someone who lives inside their comfort zone, much less someone who pursues a dream!

"It is impossible to live without failing at something, unless you live so cautiously that you might as well not have lived at all, in which case you have failed by default."
— *J.K. ROWLING*

Fear is nothing but a state of mind, and it is the failure and setbacks we can learn from the most. As you read in the previous chapter about my arrest, our mistakes serve as lessons of wisdom and the only mistakes we truly make are the ones we don't learn from.

Even during an experience that is seemingly negative, frustrating, and appears to be a major setback, always remember that you are a wiser person for having experienced it.

Think of your mind as fertile soil and your thoughts as seeds. When we allow bad thoughts to consume our minds, we are subconsciously planting bad seeds. And these bad seeds can grow into bad plants.

Bad seeds = Bad thoughts.

In contrast, what grows in your mental soil when you plant good seeds? Good plants, of course.

Good seeds = Good thoughts.

Good or bad, your thinking is a result of what seeds receive your focus. And, as with plants, you will reap what you sow!

Remind yourself often of your greatest accomplishments, especially when you encounter obstacles and frustrations. The frustrations will be there—expect them. But so will the benefits if you remember to turn the frustrations into learning experiences.

Your mental focus dictates how you feel, and how you feel dictates how you act. So, focus on finding the positive and, even when it seems invisible, you will find it. Again, remind yourself of your past achievements because they are proof that the possibility of success is not just wishful thinking. No one is ever defeated until they believe they are defeated.

"Many of life's failures are people who did not realize how close they were to success when they gave up."
— *THOMAS A. EDISON*

To watch my TEDx talk where I share my research and discovery about what all great leaders have in common, visit http://kevincsnyder.com/free-stuff (16 min)

• *BEFORE YOU GO* •

Before moving on to the next chapter, take a moment to reflect on how you feel right now so you can return to review your thoughts at a later date.

What did you learn from this chapter?

_____
_____
_____
_____

What surprised you?

_____
_____
_____
_____

What affirmed what you already know?

_____
_____
_____
_____

What are you now ready for?

_____
_____
_____
_____

What is something new you desire in your life?

_____
_____
_____
_____

Turning Point

"You are not *what* you think you are;
rather, what you *think*, you are."
— *ANCIENT PROVERB*

I grew up in North Carolina with a brother, sister, and two great, loving parents. I vividly remember sixth grade—having lots of friends and "going with" several girls. When I was that age, "going with" was the precursor to dating. I felt like a rock star.

For me, sixth grade was more fun and social than educational. My parents had to limit the number of phone calls I received at night, and they ordered a second phone line just because I was constantly on the first phone line. These were the days before cell phones!

Fast forward to seventh grade. I dated "Crystal" and truly felt a junior high love crush for the first time. In fact, I liked Crystal so much that I wrote "I Love Crystal" on my blue Chucks shoes and on my desk in each class.

Crystal and I had been dating for six months, which in seventh grade is equivalent to forty-nine dog years, when one day she had a friend of hers break up with me in the cafeteria during lunch—in front of everyone. Obviously, our breakup took me by surprise. I was devastated and cried in front of all my friends. I ran to the bathroom and stayed there for the entire lunch.

The next class period, I saw Crystal walking down the hallway holding hands with my best friend, John. I could not believe it! I was devastated.

I charged John, intending to punch him to the ground. Luckily, for both of us, another friend held me back.

The next few days were painful. All I could think about was Crystal and why she broke up with me. I also constantly wondered why John would do such a thing to me.

At the time, I felt I was not good enough for either of them. I remember wanting to be different for Crystal—that is, more like my best friend—so she might like *me* again. For the first time that I could remember in my life, I was facing rejection ... and this was only the beginning.

2nd grade

For the next several weeks, I faced even more rejection. My popularity seemed to diminish, and phone calls at night almost stopped. All of a sudden, I didn't feel like one of the coolest kids in school anymore. Moreover, I got cut during soccer team tryouts, a sport I loved and had played my entire life. I was really good at soccer, so none of this made sense to me.

My life had changed suddenly and drastically, all outside of my control.

A few weeks later, I saw Crystal at a friend's birthday party. We spoke later that evening. As we were talking she used her index finger to touch my stomach. Her exact words were, "Gaining a little bit of weight, aren't we?"

6th grade

Her comment stuck with me, and my mind kept repeating her words over and over.

Maybe if I lost some *weight*, she would like me again. Maybe if I lost some *weight*, I would be more popular again. Maybe my *weight* was a factor in being cut from the soccer team too.

I became convinced that my *weight* was the major source of rejection in all areas. It was to blame for everything.

So, even at that young age, losing weight became a central focus point for me, and I assumed it would help me regain control of my life.

I didn't tell anyone, including my family, that I was going to lose weight. I just secretly started trying. But I was not successful at it. I would eat the wrong foods at the wrong times, and it was hard to keep my focus on a healthy lifestyle. For about six months, I went back and forth, losing and gaining ten or fifteen pounds each time in very unhealthy ways.

Since I hadn't made the soccer team, I tried out for wrestling. I was pretty good in my weight class of 110 pounds, but the main thing I learned from other wrestlers during that wrestling season was all about diet and how to control my weight. I mastered the ability to manage my weight before wrestling matches by eating or not eating the right things, exercising or not exercising. As a result, my weight consistently remained just under 110.

Then, just before the season was over, I decided to lose weight, hoping to look and feel better about myself. By this time, losing weight was something I knew how to do.

I remember losing five or ten pounds and feeling good. At this same time, I received compliments from people that I looked great. Crystal approached me one day and commented that I looked good. I associated my weight with everything—popularity, Crystal giving me attention again, and feeling good about myself in general.

I convinced myself that I needed to lose more weight in order to feel even better and get even more attention. Losing weight was like a drug for me—addictive—and this is when my disordered behavior began. I would have Diet Coke for breakfast, three apples for lunch, skip dinner meals, exercise continuously at odd times of the day and night, isolate myself from friends around food, and so forth.

What started as dieting led to a preoccupation with food and exercise, which further led to destructive and unhealthy behavior, which led to self-esteem and body image problems, which ultimately led to my eating disorder.

The next several months were very dark, as if my conscious thought processes had shut down. I do not remember much. I do remember constantly exercising, refusing to eat, and removing myself from any social interaction.

If I knew I would be at family dinner, that would be

the only meal I would eat all day. Of course, my parents did not realize this. I would also run and exercise before my parents even woke up in the morning, usually at 5 a.m. I followed that with at least 500 sit-ups and push-ups. This behavior and my dark spiral continued without anyone really knowing what was going on—including me.

My mom told me a story several years ago about when she first realized something was wrong. She recalled seeing me from a distance while at church, yet not recognizing me at first because I was so skinny. It was at that moment she acknowledged I had lost too much weight and something was terribly wrong. My parents finally connected the dots.

During school the very next day, my mom secretly came to school and had me called to the principal's office. I remember this vividly—it was third period Algebra, and the principal's secretary called my name over the intercom in class. All my classmates thought I was getting in trouble. I was shocked as well. What had I done?

I was surprised to see my mom when I arrived at the office. She was crying. She had come to take me to the doctor and assumed I would be extremely angry. Surprising both of us, however, I didn't say a word.

As we walked out, I noticed a security officer around the corner. Mom told me she was taking me to the doctor because she was concerned about my health. Again, I didn't say a word. I just walked to the car alongside her. The security officer was right behind me. I learned years later that he was there to catch me if I tried to run away.

When I was weighed at the doctor's office, I weighed 76 pounds which was 29 pounds lighter than three months prior. My pulse was 49 beats per minute, and the doctor was extremely worried.

The doctor asked if I had ever heard of "anorexia nervosa." I had not, and it didn't sound good. I remember feeling very confused.

The doctor then informed my mom, with me standing next to her, that I had anorexia nervosa and should be admit-

ted to a hospital immediately for treatment. The doctor emphatically stressed that my body could not safely lose another ounce and that if I did lose more weight, I was at risk of severe long-term complications and possibly death. The doctor told my mom that if I didn't gain weight immediately, I might die.

8th grade

Hearing those words of gaining weight terrified me. I felt sick to my stomach. I was scared.

I told my mom I was *not* going to some hospital because, if I did, all my friends would know I had some sort of "problem." The irony was lost on me at the time that all anyone had to do was look at me to know I was emaciated. As you see in the above photo—taken for our annual school yearbook just one day before my mom took me to the doctor— I looked like a skeleton.

While the doctor and my parents investigated

hospitals and treatment centers, I was allowed to stay at home as long as I agreed to counseling and tried to regain my weight. This is when my battle really began. I had to force myself to eat.

Gaining weight was completely against the lifestyle I had developed. Even grasping the severity of my condition, I still did not recognize the importance of eating—I was terrified of calories, and the mental image of putting any "fat" at all back on my body was beyond horrifying.

A few years ago, my dad recalled a conversation he had with me during this dark time. He had asked me what it was about food that scared me. He said my response was:

> *"Dad, just being near food is like standing on the edge of a pool filled with hungry sharks ... eating food is like being pushed in."*

My life continued to spiral out of control as I began the treatment process and had to face my fear of eating food to gain weight. Every day after school my mom would pick me up and take me to psychologists, psychiatrists, nutritionists, weigh-ins at the doctor's office, and other doctors who wanted to study my then-rare condition.

How my mother had time for this I still do not know, but she taxied me around every afternoon after school. We usually would not get home until right before dinner—this was my life for over six months. Doctors, doctors, weigh-ins, doctors ...

In the meantime, there were no hospitals available to me. There were eating disorder centers for females but not males. There were clinics for adults but not adolescents. There were centers for juveniles with behavioral and legal problems but none were focused on eating disorders. Being a male, juvenile, anorexic, my condition did not fit any of these places, so I continued being treated while living at home.

Again, I don't remember much during this dark time of my life. Maybe my subconscious does not want me to remember, or maybe my body and mind just shut down and didn't retain many memories.

For the first several weeks, my sessions with the psychologist were completely silent. I would sit there staring at the floor, feeling that the session was a waste of my time. I would not say a word. The counselor would let me sit there, asking me a question every fifteen minutes or so, hoping, I suppose, to spark a conversation.

The weigh-ins at the doctor's office were even more difficult. After all, I was supposed to be gaining weight. If at any time my weight dropped, the doctor threatened to send me to a treatment facility in another state. I did not want that, so I would try various things to keep the scales at least in the same place. I remember once drinking nearly a gallon of water just before a weigh-in because I knew I was a few pounds lighter that day. My stomach felt like it might burst, but I just could not let the doctor catch me at a lighter weight.

Finally, one day, I broke down during one of my counseling sessions. It was the first time I actually spoke to the psychologist in months. I cried. I screamed at her. I said I hated being there. I asked how long I would have to keep coming, saying that all I wanted was to be "normal" again and that I didn't feel normal being there because it only reminded that I had a problem. My psychologist didn't give me a direct answer but just let me rant.

That same day, riding in the back seat of our van while my mom drove me home, I opened the side door and put one foot out, preparing to jump. I was so angry and out of control that I just wanted to end my life.

My mom screamed and, at 65 miles an hour, slammed on the brakes, throwing me hard against the front seat but saving my life as the van came to a stop.

That night I couldn't sleep. In fact, during this whole dark period, I had clinical insomnia, sleeping maybe two or three hours a night. Routinely, I would go to bed near ten or eleven, but my mind would be racing with all sorts of issues such as exercise, what foods to eat or not eat the next day, how I would eat it, how much fat was on my body, and how I was going to secretly exercise.

Everything changed that night. Around two in the morning, my mom must have heard me crying. She came in my room and sat down on my bed. I didn't say anything but just cried even more.

I finally said to her, "I can't go on like this. I hate my life. I just want to be normal again." After a few moments she said, "You're going to get better, honey. Please continue to be strong." We cried together for a few more minutes, and then I fell asleep.

That particular day would turn out to be the most important day of my life. I had finally hit rock bottom.

After yelling at my psychologist, nearly committing

suicide by jumping out of a speeding car on a busy highway, and breaking down emotionally with my mother, I woke up the next morning ready to admit that I was not going to get better until I made some changes. I desperately wanted to regain both my health and control of my life. As terrifying as I knew it would be, I decided to accept the fact that I had to change in some way. I wasn't even sure what that meant, but I knew I needed to do something. And in that moment, my recovery process began. Otherwise, I knew I would die either from taking my own life or my body just giving up.

• *TURNING POINT* •

I still performed my normal routine of exercising before and after breakfast, but I felt motivated to get healthy again. With each passing day, I started feeling better. That was my sole goal in life so I could feel "normal" again.

I still struggled with food and feared fat on my body, but I knew that gaining weight was the only way I could reclaim a normal life. I worked on changing my neuro-association with food, meaning I proactively worked to convert my mental association with food from one of "fear" to one of "healthy and normal." I had to remind myself that food was not the enemy but rather was part of the equation to make me better.

Over the next several months, I gained about half a pound each week. I continued my workouts but with a goal to put the weight back on in the right places. My doctor, my counselor, and my parents were all okay with my workouts as long as I was gaining weight.

Once my weight rose to 86 pounds, I told the doctor

I wanted to wrestle again. Even though he was proud of me for gaining 10 pounds, he denied my request. However, he and my mom both agreed that if I reached 95 pounds, I would be allowed to join the wrestling team.

Gaining nine more pounds—just enough to get back on the wrestling team—became my goal. In fact, it became my obsession. I drank three 1,000 calorie protein shakes a day and I gained those nine pounds in just two weeks.

The doctor was proud of me and immediately wrote an approval note to my wrestling coach. I went to practice the next day and joined the 95-pound weight class.

Three other guys were in the same weight class, so I had to beat them in order to start on the team. Within the next week, I wrestled each of them during practice—and beat them all. At the wrestling match the following week, I was the starter for the 95-pound weight class!

My mom and dad were extremely happy for me— they were also shocked. Even for me, this experience was surreal. I had set a goal to wrestle again and, suddenly, despite all the heartache of the last several months, I was better than ever. Thanks to my workouts, I was actually in perfect shape. What's more, I had gained the weight back in a healthy manner.

That next wrestling match was against our arch rival school. It was a big match, and the gym was packed full of people. My mom and dad both came to watch me compete.

I later found out that my coach had called my parents the night before that match to tell them I was wrestling the best wrestler in the conference. He wanted to prepare my parents because, after all the months I'd been out of the game, the coach didn't expect me to win. In fact, he expected me to get beat terribly and he had no clue how I'd react to a defeat like that.

He and my parents were all uncertain how I would handle the defeat. But to everyone's surprise—perhaps mine, most of all—no one had to find out.

I won my match! When I left the wrestling mat, coach hugged me and happily informed me that I had just defeated an "undefeated" wrestler who was the previous year's conference champion!

That remaining season I dominated every remaining match, remaining undefeated and even winning the conference championship and a gold medal. I advanced to the state competition and got third place in that tournament.

Despite the negative press that wrestling often receives, wrestling gave me a positive focus. It was an activity I looked forward to each day. I truly believe wrestling redirected my focus away from food and helped me become focused toward a positive goal.

We all need a positive focus. In my case, a positive focus saved my life.

My recovery continued to be an uphill battle, but I recognized—and gave myself credit for—each week's improvement. Some days were better than others, but my life finally seemed back in control.

As I grew older, I pushed this chapter of my life to the back of my mind. Having anorexia was not an experience I was proud of, and I just wanted to forget it. It wasn't until I began motivational speaking that I realized how my story could help others.

One of my favorite portions of each keynote presentation is talking to audience members afterward. I love hearing their stories and which of my messages in each presentation best connected with them. I continue to be amazed at how many people open up to me about their personal struggles after hearing mine.

If I can serve one role for anyone battling any mental illness—whether that is you, someone you know, or someone in general—my purpose is to reassure anyone they are not alone. There is hope.

I somehow found hope on the same day when I wanted to end my own life. And if it wasn't for my amazing mom who facilitated an intervention, I am certain I would not have lived to write this book.

For these reasons, I share my painful life experiences with my audiences and readers, like you. I believe my stories can impact the lives of others and model a pathway to lead them toward healing, resilience, and recovery. If I could beat my disease, surely there is hope for others as well. I've given new meaning to my battles and I aspire to use my experiences for good.

**"Nothing has meaning except
the meaning we give it."
— KEVIN C. SNYDER**

For those of you who might be struggling with an eating disorder, please talk with a professional. I know it is difficult to reach out, and you may have to hit rock bottom first, like I did, before you acknowledge the severity of your condition, but your life depends on facing your reality.

If you find yourself in this situation, please make the positive choice to talk with a professional and find help. This is truly the only way to get better and become healthy.

I was lucky. During that time in my life, I did not even recognize the dark depression I was in. My parents had to step in and make sure I got help before it was too late. I certainly would not have stopped the cycle on my own. Looking back, I realize that even by the time my mom took me to the doctor, I was near death. If she hadn't taken action, I would have died.

My school picture from that year shows how devastating my condition was. It's shocking to me now that no one called my parents to inquire about me or my health. It's alarming that no one pulled me aside and asked what was wrong. Would I have needed to die in order for people to notice something was wrong with me? There is a problem here, and it needs to be addressed.

However, my downward spiral was stopped because someone did step in. I eventually began the healing process, though it took months before progress even started. But when I finally understood the *power of mindset*, I felt reborn. I'm also extremely thankful and blessed that I have a platform for speaking and writing so that I can share my story and message with people like you. I hope you will use my story for good and be the ripple effect for yourself and others. It's not too late.

If you know someone who is struggling with anorexia, depression, or any type of addiction, please help them. Show them you care. They may not yet be ready to help themselves, and you may need to take the first step for them, or first five steps, the way my mom did for me. You will need to be brave to help them. One idea is to give them a copy of this book! Let them read for themselves my story of survival and recovery.

Think about it this way ... if you don't help them, who will? And what will likely happen if no one helps them?

"If not you, then who? If not now, then when?"
— *ANDRZEJ KOLIKOWSKI*

As I mentioned before, I also believe that wrestling played a critical role in my recovery. It was more than just a sport for me. Wrestling was symbolic of the importance for goal setting. It was reflective of my desire to get healthy, and I gave it 110 percent. When I conquered wrestling, I conquered anorexia. When I was awarded the gold medal at the conference tournament, in my heart I felt I was awarded the gold medal for beating anorexia.

I am not a medical doctor, and I am most certainly not a medical expert on eating disorders. However, I am an expert on the struggles I endured, on my survival and recovery, and on how I can make reason of my life experience.

I do not agree with the popular phrase, "Things happen for a reason." Rather, I prefer, "You have to make reason out of the things that happen."

Anorexia nervosa, as with all eating disorders, is a serious mental disease. Studies have found that complications from eating disorders kill nearly 20 percent of those diagnosed. Eating disorders are also the third most common chronic illnesses among adolescent women.

Healthy bodies come in all shapes and sizes. We don't need to change our bodies; we need to change our attitudes. People can and do recover from eating disorders. If you are struggling with an eating disorder, I hope my story inspires you to talk with a professional counselor. If you know someone struggling with an eating disorder, go with them to talk with a professional counselor. The longer the symptoms are ignored or denied, the more difficult recovery will be.

For more information about identifying eating disorders, prevention, and how you can help, please visit any of the following web sites:

www.nationaleatingdisorders.org
www.bulimia.com
www.nami.org

• BEFORE YOU GO •

Before moving on to the next chapter, take a moment to reflect on how you feel right now so you can return to review your thoughts at a later date.

What did you learn from this chapter?

_____

_____

_____

_____

What surprised you?

_____

_____

_____

_____

What affirmed what you already know?

_____

_____

_____

_____

What are you now ready for?

_____

_____

_____

_____

What is something new you desire in your life?

_____

_____

_____

_____

The Secret

"**Whatever it is that you are feeling is a perfect reflection of what it is you are becoming.**"
— *RHONDA BYRNE*

Have you heard of the phenomena called *The Secret*? It's a concept that bloomed in the mid-2000s and was both a film and book. *The Secret* was so successful that many experts were projecting it to be the most successful personal development program in history.

To watch "The Secret" inspirational movie clip, visit http://kevincsnyder.com/free-stuff (6 min)

Still intrigued to know what *The Secret* is? I wish I could share it with you but unfortunately I can't, because after all, it's a secret.

... okay, kidding! Actually, not only will I share with you some of the philosophy explained in *The Secret*, I will

THINK DIFFERENTLY

introduce my interpretation of how it will change your life once it is understood and applied.

• WHAT IS *THE SECRET*? •

The author of *The Secret,* Rhonda Byrne, has based the concept primarily upon the Law of Attraction, which she describes as a universal law suggesting that *like attracts like.* Everything in the world—or universe, as she puts it—is comprised of energy, and this energy attracts *like* energy. For example, as we think good thoughts and feel good, we resultantly attract more good things into our lives.

The opposite (but same!) result happens when we focus on negative thoughts and feelings: we attract correspondingly negative circumstances into our lives. So, in its simplicity, *The Secret* says you get what you focus on, good or bad. Sound familiar?

The Secret had people talking as if it were a discovery just found in a deep abyss. In reality, its principles can be found in most teachings of any past or present inspirational speaker, success coach, or motivational author, including yours truly. For example, Anthony Robbins, Norman Vincent Peale, Wayne Dyer, and Zig Ziglar all have expressed and taught a concurring belief system that explains (1) when we know what we want, (2) are focused, committed, and passionate about it truly happening, and (3) take persistent action toward this goal, then (4) we will manifest our desires.

Principals from *The Secret* can also be found in the

Bible. Books that *The Secret* credits as being influential include *As a Man Thinketh* and *Think and Grow Rich,* both of which I have cited throughout this book.

As you might sense from my interpretation of *The Secret,* I do not consider this philosophy to be such a secret! However, I do validate its intentional, *brilliantly marketed,* and well-articulated message that challenges us to awaken and bring about the personal power that already lies within each of us. Its concept is much more than just "positive thinking." It is positive *believing.*

"Our brains become magnetized with the dominating thoughts which we hold in our minds. These 'magnets' attract to us the forces, the people, the circumstances of life which harmonize with the nature of our dominating thoughts."
— *NAPOLEON HILL*, THINK AND GROW RICH

• APPLYING *THE SECRET* •

Your greatest dreams cannot manifest in your life until you invite them. The philosophy shared in *The Secret* challenges each of us to identify and awaken our forgotten dreams and unpursued goals. Remember your proudest accomplishment I asked you to identify from the prior chapter? Did this happen by accident or was it a result of your belief and persistent action? Whether you realize it or not, you already know *The Secret*!

For just a moment, think about a personal or professional goal you have. If this goal seems extreme or ridiculous, go with it anyway. It has to be a goal you truly desire and believe in. More importantly, it must be one about which you are passionate! (You read about PASSION earlier!) Do not focus on "how" you will manifest this goal in your life. The "how" will show up—if you truly *believe*.

As *Chicken Soup for the Soul* co-author Jack Canfield explains in *The Secret*, you should equate the "how" of your goals with driving your car at night. When you drive at night, your headlights only reveal the next 200 feet of road in front of your car. Yet you can confidently drive from California to New York while seeing only 200 feet of road at a time because you know the road is there even though it is, for the moment, out of sight. Having confidence that the road is there gives you the faith to keep driving.

Again, do not focus on or wait to figure out the "how" for achieving your identified goal. The "how" will become clearer as you proceed. For now, just believe in the reality of your goal and take those first steps toward it. Your subconscious and conscious mind will work together to bring it to you.

Write your desire below:

_____

_____

_____

_____

_____

_____

Now that you have identified your goal, visualize yourself already accomplishing and receiving it. Focus on it already happening in your life.

I mean this quite literally. Close your eyes and visualize this goal and desire as being present in your life. See your goal clearly in your mind and in specific detail. If your goal is something tangible, envision touching it. How does it feel? What color is it? If your goal is an experience or accomplishment, envision you are in process of achieving it. What specifically are you doing? Where are you? If your goal is financial or business related, what specifically is it? How are you measuring your success? Is it an award, an amount, etc.? If your goal is relationship or family oriented, describe it in your mind. What does it look like? How does it feel to have that outcome in your life?

Just as the Law of Attraction promises, if you complete the activity with clarity and detail, and you truly, truly *envision* your goal, you will begin to attract your outcome like a magnet and manifest it in your life. And remember, there is a crucial difference between *hope* and *expectancy*. You can't simply *hope* your goal will happen. You must *know* that it will happen. *Envision* it, *knowing* it *will* manifest.

This is the part of dream visualization that most people do not understand or that they shy away from. Some people feel foolish trying it even when they are alone. And because they do not understand it or are reluctant to try it, they never see the potential it has to enhance their life.

If you tried the exercise above and visualized your desire correctly and without distraction, your chest should be full of energy right now. If you do not feel this, then repeat the activity. This energy is the emotion and state of mind you must capture as you transform your goal into a vision and begin to take action. Remember, *like* attracts *like*!

Try this exercise repeatedly in a setting where you can be focused. Results may not happen overnight (though they might!), but with persistence, you will eventually feel and see progress. Repeat this exercise for every desire you wish to pursue.

As you intentionally focus on unwavering success and continually improve upon methods that work well for you, you will become incredibly powerful. Your positive energy becomes magnetic and attracts positive circumstances. By exercising the personal power within your mind, you can manifest your personal and professional goals in a matter of time.

DISCLAIMER:
The Law of Attraction only works
for people who believe it will!

• *BEFORE YOU GO* •

Before moving on to the next chapter, take a moment to reflect on how you feel right now so you can return to review your thoughts at a later date.

What did you learn from this chapter?

_____

_____

_____

_____

What surprised you?

_____

_____

_____

_____

What affirmed what you already know?

_____

_____

_____

_____

What are you now ready for?

_____

_____

_____

_____

What is something new you desire in your life?

_____

_____

_____

_____

More to
The Secret

"When you desire a change or something new in your life, be sure your actions aren't contradicting your desires. Only aligned actions can properly send out a signal of expectation for you to receive it!" — *RHONDA BYRNE*

A s often as I share the philosophy behind *The Secret*, I am routinely confronted by people who say it will not work or that it is unrealistic and naïve to believe you can literally attract circumstances into your life, both desired and undesired. I usually just smile at them. I, too, remember having doubts about the Law of Attraction. Once again ...

DISCLAIMER:
The Law of Attraction only works for people who believe it will!

But when I put *The Secret* to the ultimate test, my life not only changed for the better, it *soared!* I became an unstoppable force, accomplishing everything I set my mind to! It's because of those successes and the new reality that I manifested in my life that I so passionately believe in its philosophy to this day.

However, contrary to what *The Secret* suggests, it is my opinion that you cannot just sit back, dream big thoughts about a Ferrari and expect a Ferrari to show up outside in your driveway. This approach *is* unrealistic and simply naïve. But a more realistic, determined approach can yield remarkable results.

Many people live by *The Secret* but just don't know it. Remember, *The Secret* is not really a "secret." It is actually an age-old philosophy that has simply been brilliantly repackaged for our day and age so anyone can understand and learn from it.

A few years ago, Oprah Winfrey had several of *The Secret's* main philosophers as guests on her television show. During the interview, even Oprah admitted she had always lived by the same "positive believing" philosophy they were describing but that she did not call it a secret! She also acknowledged not understanding the science behind the philosophy.

I felt the same as Oprah back then. It took me a while before I finally realized the importance of adding visualization to the goal-setting process. That is, I did not at first recognize that perhaps the "thought" and "vision" processes were just as important as the "action" process and that the equation for achieving extreme levels of success might be based on the interdependence of these factors.

"Anything the mind can believe, it can conceive."
— THOMAS EDISON

"All goals in life must first begin with a dream."
— WALT DISNEY

"Nothing will change in your life until you make a change about how you think about it."
— WAYNE DYER

Think about my *Price is Right* story (Chapter 2) for just a moment. Was it luck that I met Chris? Was it luck that I got called down to *Contestants' Row*? Was it luck that I lived my dream? Or was the Law of Attraction at work in my life even before I understood it existed?

You see, living my dream of being on *The Price is Right* all started with a seed of desire—more simply, a goal.

That goal quickly became a vision of expectation because I desired it so strongly. I *knew* without any doubt that I would eventually be shaking hands with Bob Barker on that national television stage.

One step further, I remember my vision being so vivid in my mind that I could already watch myself on my own mental television set long before it ever happened. It was only a matter of time despite me not knowing "how" it would happen.

Then I took physical action to make things happen. I faithfully watched and studied the show. I studied prices of grocery items, furniture, and cars. I traveled cross-country to California—twice! I didn't listen to the naysayers who laughed at me and told me my dream was crazy. Instead, I listened to my heart. I listened to my desire. And then I met someone so randomly—Chris—who told me exactly *how* to get on the show when I was finally *ready* to be on the show.

So, no, living my dream was not luck. Living my dream of being on *The Price is Right* was a testimony of my own faith, my positive belief system, and the Law of Attraction in full effect.

You too can live a dream if you haven't already. I'm living proof it's possible. You just have to believe in yourself and trust that this process works. Why not try it out? Put it to the test as you'll read how I did in this chapter.

Perhaps you're currently living a dream and you want to live a few more dreams. This process will ensure you get there quicker and you'll enjoy the journey. Or perhaps you used to have a dream but life has become too complicated and you had to put your dream on hold for a while.

How long has "a while" been for you? Years? Decades? Listen, I understand and greatly respect the reality of priority precedence. If your parent or child is sick, if you're paycheck to paycheck, or life just seems too daunting right now, I truly understand. But please, don't ever convince yourself you don't have time to start living your dream. If now isn't the right time, think about when the right time will be. Otherwise it'll never happen. It'll be five years—maybe ten or 20 years—from now before you know it. So if you keep putting your dream on hold, you'll be putting *you* on hold. And when you put you on hold, everything around you is indirectly impacted. You'll never be living your full potential. You also won't be inspiring others to reach their full potential if they don't see you inspired first!

Would you advise a child to put their dream on hold? Or would you encourage the child to find his or her passion, start small, and follow the dream?

From my travels speaking to hundreds of thousands of people and getting emails from thousands upon thousands of people ranging from young students to corporate executives and all in between, I commonly hear that people either don't know what their dream is or that they didn't even realize they had put their dream on hold. I always respond, and I refer them back to various portions of this book depending on what they wrote me. I know the content in this book can help change lives because people have told me it's changed theirs.

I absolutely love hearing from people (hint! ***Kevin@ KevinCSnyder.com***), so contact me and share your story. If I can help provide more information that encourages you specifically, do not for one second hesitate to reach out to me. And as you're reading this book, tag me on social media so I can respond to your comment: ***@KevinCSnyder***.

If you're not listening to your desires and pursuing your passion now, there will be a day when you wake up and you wish you had started yesterday. There will be a day when you wake up feeling stuck. There will be a day when you want more. There will be a day when you need more from a relationship. There will be a day.

Why not let that day be today? Allow this book to be a catalyst in your own thinking. This book has come into your life for a reason. *The Law of Attraction is already working in your life because you are holding this book*!

Whoever you are and wherever you might be in your life, the beautiful, simple truth is that you're exactly in the perfect place to start now. I'm honored that this book might be the "Miracle Grow" on the mental seeds you'll be planting. I am humbled to be part of your journey, and I look forward to hearing about how your life will change.

But as Wayne Dyer said, "Nothing will change in your life until you make a change about how you think about it." One step further, nothing will change in your life until you decide to do something about it!

Without the action components to live my dream of being on *The Price is Right* happen, I would still be sitting in my living room watching the television rather than having already been on it!

> **"There are three types of people in this world: those who make things happen, those who watch things happen, and those who wonder what happened."** — *MARY KAY ASH*

When I read *The Secret*, I reflected on my *Price is Right* experience and realized that something greater than I had been silently at work back then to manifest that dream into my life—the Law of Attraction and my faith. So, with *The Secret* fresh in my mind, I decided to test the philosophy by creating a vision board, defining a few more goals that were just as extreme as—maybe even more than—my dream of being on *The Price is Right*!

The Secret introduces the powerful concept of a "vision board," which is literally a collage of visual imagery representing your desires, goals, declarations, and dreams. The images are symbolic of what you truly want in your life and what you passionately expect to attract into your life. The board can be in the form of a corkboard, a large poster, or it can be as simple as a sheet of paper, a computer screensaver, or whatever works best for you.

My vision board was, and still is, very simple. For my first board, I clipped photos from magazines, I typed phrases and specific goals on paper that I then cut out. All these, I simply glued onto a fluorescent orange poster board. My board wasn't necessarily pretty but it reflected my true desires and things I honestly saw myself achieving in the months and years ahead.

That is Rule #1 for your vision board: you must

passionately believe in *everything* you put on it. It's a "vision board," not a "hope board." Paste goals you actually envision manifesting in your future and be very specific.

One of the items I put on my vision board related to a job promotion. I included the date for that new job and the salary I was going to earn in that new job. Another set of images related to a partnership with a speakers bureau. I typed and cut out phrases about being accepted into a Doctoral program, the year of my completion date for the Doctorate, and "Tuition PAID For!" Rounding out my goals, I included imagery regarding a dog leash invention I had been working on and, last but not least, the publication of *this book* you are reading now.

Again, it is essential that you realize my goals were truly "visions" when I put them on my vision board. I believed in them and saw them in my life, but they were still only dreams in my mind. And quite frankly, some of them were beyond my comfort zone. I had no clue "how" they were going to manifest into my life, but I chose to believe that they would, and so they went on my vision board.

One more time ...

DISCLAIMER:
The Law of Attraction only works for people who believe it will!

Within one year of making that first vision board, here's what happened:

I accepted that new dream job with nearly the same title I listed on my board.

I received a salary within $1,000 of what I'd posted.

I became a professional speaker with a speaking bureau called CAMPUSPEAK.

I was admitted into a Doctorate program.

And, I was informed by the Vice President of my university that my doctorate program would be "PAID For" if I accepted my job promotion.

Are you freakin' kidding me?! My test worked! Folks, this is how the Law of Attraction works. Start with your vision board as soon as possible!

It had been fun to play around with the vision board idea and treat the concept like yet another game. But then my "test" to see if the vision board concept worked proved the concept true!

But wait—that's not all. The best example is still to come!

Four years before I read and learned about *The Secret* and vision board activity, I had an idea about a way to improve the everyday dog leash. When my dogs—a lab named Guinness and an English bulldog named Snuka—were puppies, I would take them for walks only to be frustrated that their retractable leash lines would constantly become entangled. I would generally spend half our walks untangling their leash lines.

I began shopping around for a dual, retractable leash that would solve my problem. I went to all the retail pet stores, veterinarians, and online stores, and I investigated any other likely looking source, but I found nothing close to what I was after.

I finally realized that I was going to have to make the

product I needed. Years prior, I had thought about inventions and realized that most inventions solve common, everyday problems, so I thought to myself, "Why not *invent* the product I need?"

I started by researching the concept of multi-dog pet leashes. I spent hours on the Internet and visiting pet stores, making sure that my pet leash idea didn't already exist. After clicking to what felt like the end of the Internet and traveling hundreds of miles visiting stores and speaking with managers, I felt confident my idea did *not* exist. I could not find any comparable product. It was compelling to me that the people I did inquire with thought what I was looking for was a great idea. I also performed several patent searches and hired a patent attorney to help me protect my idea.

But even though my idea was crystal clear in my head, I had no clue how to actually make a physical version. I mentally envisioned walking two dogs simultaneously, but I had no clue how the internal component parts comprising the leash would actually function. Although I knew it could be done, the "how" of my leash concept was the obstacle I could not figure out.

I allowed myself to get in my own way. And as a result, my invention was put on hold. Six months later, my idea was still on hold. Even though I thought about it frequently, all I did was *think about it*! I could never figure out how to actually make the internal components to the leash. The frustration was beginning to build.

You see what was happening here? The "how" of my idea was getting in my way.

In hindsight (which, as we all know, has 20/20 vision!), I realized I was focusing my energy on not knowing how to create my invention rather than on attracting the circumstances to get it created. If only I had understood the power of the Law of Attraction back then!

One year went by. Then two. Then another. No leash. When folks asked how the project was going, I always had excuses ready to explain why the leash still did *not* exist—I was too busy in my job, patents were too expensive, my speaking career was taking off, my Doctorate program was too intense, I didn't know how to make it, etc.

I was more creative in finding excuses why things weren't progressing than I was in identifying solutions to my problems. Sound familiar?

But then—four years after conceiving the leash idea—enter *The Secret* and the vision board concept. When I added the dog leash invention to my vision board, things immediately began to change. With rekindled interest, I made the choice to re-pursue the leash idea once again. The difference this time was *action* and a change in attitude. I shifted my focus away from excuses and redirected it toward all the reasons why I should pursue the leash invention.

Exactly six days after pasting the phrase, "No-Tangle Multi-Dog Leash," on my vision board, a student of mine (Mike) at the university came to see me in my office. He asked me if I had ever wanted to invent something.

I stared at Mike in utter disbelief.

I asked Mike what he was interested in inventing. He said he didn't have a specific idea, but he felt I might. He had heard a rumor I had been working on something.

It turned out that Mike was one of the best computer design students at the university. He was also an engineering physics major which meant he had the brains and computer skills I had been in need of ever since I conceived the idea for my invention. Mike, like Chris in my *The Price is Right* story, was the "how" of my dream.

That very next weekend, Mike and I got together. I brought several single retractable leashes with me just so we could break them apart to study their internal design.

To my amazement, within just a few hours we drew the internal components for the leash concept I had envisioned and dreamed about. As I continued to work on the business plan and reach out to prospective investors, Mike's role for the next few weeks was to electronically draft the design of the leash on his computer.

A dream I had procrastinated about for four years had, in only a few hours, became a reality. Mike was the missing link, and he arrived in my life just as soon as I decided to put the leash on the vision board and commit to the idea.

THE STORY CONTINUES ...

The very next weekend, I was at a nearby restaurant with some friends. I was introduced to a woman with whom I felt an immediate energy and connection. After talking with her for several minutes, I asked her what she did for a living. She replied, "I am a distributor for pet supplies."

I almost fainted. She had no clue I had just invented

a redesigned dog leash. Once Mike and I created the leash, she could be the distributor who might help us sell it.

Two weeks after meeting the woman who distributed pet supplies, I received a phone message from a friend who is a flight attendant. She was calling to offer me her "Buddy Pass," which meant I could fly stand-by for free to anywhere her airline flies. What a bonus to my plans! Now, when I needed to travel to exhibit my dog leash to executives and companies interested in licensing it, I could fly for free!

Again, I could not believe how all this was unfolding. It was as if a red carpet had been laid out right before my eyes, showing me the way to manifest the leash and become amazingly successful.

> **"Imagination will often carry us to worlds**
> **that never were. But without it we go nowhere."**
> **— CARL SAGAN, AMERICAN ASTRONOMER**
> **AND ASTROCHEMISt**

This leash story is just another surreal and exciting example of how you can make anything happen in your life as long as you believe in it enough, are passionate enough, and are willing to make the choice to see it through.

Interested in seeing what a No-Tangle looks like?
Simply do a Google search for Freedom Leash™!

It is simple to create your own vision board. First, think of all the things you desire out of life. Write down whatever comes to your mind ...

- What do you seek?
- Do you feel anything is missing in your life?
- What would make you feel happier?
- What desires are in your heart?
- Where do you dream of living?
- Do you dream of being married?
- Dream of having children? If so, how many?
- What would make you feel truly fulfilled?
- What are your goals? Write them and be very specific!
- Where do you see yourself spiritually, financially, and in your career within one year? Five years? Ten years?
- Describe the type of health you aspire to have.
- What is the title of your dream job? Type it up and paste on your board!
- What salary or income do you expect to have? Type it up!
- Describe the type of relationship you want to be in.
- Describe how the person in that relationship looks. Find an image of them and paste it on your board.
- What type of home do you want to live in? Find a picture of it!
- Describe your lifestyle.
- What types of hobbies do you want to pursue?
- Describe your overall happiness.
- Etc., etc., etc.!

But remember, you must be *as specific as possible*. The key is for you to identify and focus on your desires. Find a quiet spot for a few hours and listen to your mind tell you exactly what it desires. You likely will need several sessions of doing this before you have clarity and are ready to begin creating your physical vision board.

Once you feel you have enough desires listed for what you want and what you expect to manifest in your future, it's time to create your first vision board. Write your vision board ideas in the space provided. Write whatever comes to your mind. Please trust this process.

And don't rush it! Take all the time you need. If you're going to continue reading this book without completing your vision board, please come back to this section. I am confident this process will help catapult your life and dreams into a new awakening of positive intention.

"Imagination is the preview to life's coming attractions." — ALBERT EINSTEIN

Also, before we continue, I must stress to you that the items you list on your inaugural vision board must be goals you believe in and are passionate about. You can't *hope* for them to arrive into your life. You must fully trust and believe that they *will*. And most importantly, don't even think about "how" they will ... just know they will for right now!

Your First Vision Board

"The people who are crazy enough to think they can change the world are the ones who do."
— *STEVE JOBS*

Items on your vision board do not have to be realistic; in fact, I hope some of them seem crazy! Don't share them with anyone else at this point unless you really want to or feel you should. Consider having someone else,

such as your partner or significant other, make their own vision board alongside you. Why not have this be a family activity?

Just keep in mind that it is imperative *you* believe in your desires and dreams so strongly that you can already visualize each one in your mind. It's only a matter of time before you start receiving them.

Download my vision board template on
www.KevinCSnyder.com/free-stuff

"There is a difference between wishing for something and being ready to receive it. No one is ready until they believe they deserve it.
The state of mind must be belief."
— JAMES ALLEN, AS A MAN THINKETH

Remember, Thomas Edison dreamed of a lamp operated by electricity before he created it. When he put his dream to action, despite 10,000 failures, he persisted until he made the electric light bulb a physical reality!

The Wright brothers dreamed of a machine that would fly through the air and, despite hundreds of unsuccessful attempts, they finally achieved flight!

You have to be convinced that it is only a matter of time before these items appear tangibly in your life. If you do not feel this strongly about items on your vision board,

either pump up your belief or remove them from your board. The board will only work if you first envision these items in your mind!

Remember, what you think about, you bring about!

Congratulations! You have just created your first vision board! Now either photocopy or tear the vision board page out of the book and for right now, just place it in an area where you will see it daily. Your vision board will serve as a reminder to you that you must continue to focus on and make efforts toward achieving the goals you have listed.

Remember though, you cannot simply sit back and expect these goals to fall into your lap. As I introduced earlier in this chapter, this is where I emphatically disagree with some of *The Secret* philosophers and their idea of how the Law of Attraction works. For this law to work and for your vision board to manifest abundance for you, your passion for the items on your board must be so strong that it *compels you to take action.*

The strength of my desire to go to California, be on *The Price Is Right* show, and meet Bob Barker *compelled* me to get a move on! So should your desires compel you to action!

As you begin making efforts, you will find that opportunities and doors will start opening for you in areas and ways you would never have expected or imagined.

> **"Courage to live our dreams isn't about knowing the entire path; it results from taking the first step to find it."** — *KEVIN C. SNYDER*

I am proud of you for completing what may well be your first vision board. It was crucial for you to begin "playing" with this mentality and positive-thinking approach in life. But the vision board you created on the page of this book is only a "baby" board.

Now I want you to make another version that is HUGE! At the office supply or art supply store, buy a large sheet of poster board in a color that inspires you. Then, with a stack of magazines and newspapers at hand, cut out phrases, clippings, and images that reflect the same messages you wrote on your baby board. Make it a board you can display with pride! Once done, be proud of your board and resolve to focus on it daily, without limitation. Remember, there are no limitations except those we allow. You can create anything that you can imagine.

Remember what Einstein said about imagination? *It's the preview to life's coming attractions!* So keep this process fun. Invite other people who are special in your life to create a board with you. You'll be planting seeds that will change your life ... and theirs!

I have two vision boards right now—a board with my wife comprising all our family goals and a professional board with all my business and financial goals. We placed the personal board in our bedroom, and I keep my professional board in my home office. Having two vision boards was something of personal preference. But for you, feel free to make one vision board—or two or three! The key is in making one and placing it in a location where you will see it daily. If you have a significant other, definitely invite them along this journey with you. They are a major component of your support and the overall success equation!

I have shared a great deal of information with you in this chapter, and perhaps it has been overwhelming. I hope you are feeling challenged because challenge breeds change and change breeds growth.

> "Change is inevitable. Growth is optional."
> — *JOHN C. MAXWELL*

I want you to believe in your goals as much as I do in mine. I want you to feel as fulfilled as I feel today. I want you to capture the power of your mental focus, and I want you to do something with it.

Self-mastery is the hardest job you will ever tackle. Once you understand it and believe that it works, teach it to someone else.

Inspiring others is true influence. That's how we spread the ripple and change the world. It starts with us. It starts with a desire. It starts with a seed inspired to grow.

• BEFORE YOU GO •

Before moving on to the next chapter, take a moment to reflect on how you feel right now so you can return to review your thoughts at a later date.

What did you learn from this chapter?

_____

_____

_____

_____

What surprised you?

_____

_____

_____

_____

What affirmed what you already know?

_____

_____

_____

_____

What are you now ready for?

_____

_____

_____

_____

What is something new you desire in your life?

_____

_____

_____

_____

Mastering the
Art of Effective
Communication

"We have two ears and one mouth for a reason."
— *Epictetus*

Communication is the foundation for both success and failure. Research from Fortune 500 companies, CEOs, business owners, and entrepreneurs all support the idea that effective communication is essential. Research also shows that poor communication is the root of all organizational breakdown.

Communication experts say that only about 10 percent of our communication is actually spoken. If this is the case, then what makes up the remaining 90 percent?

How we communicate is so much more than the words that come from our mouth. We communicate in a myriad of other ways, including our facial expressions, tone of voice, posture, smile, and more. Each of these non-verbal gestures sends and perpetuates a clear and instant message even before our words are heard or understood.

"It's not what you say, it's how you say it."
— MAE WEST

Ineffective communicators do not understand the concept of body language, let alone utilize it to their advantage. When poor communicators try to communicate, they often do so without realizing their own posture, vocal tone, and facial expressions are saying much more than their words.

I once accepted a new job before realizing I was going to be working for a boss who was an extremely poor communicator. I was not perfect either, but in the workplace if you work for someone who doesn't communicate well, then it impacts how you feel about your job and the entire office culture. You expect your seasoned supervisor to be at least professional. Besides, how could they get that far if they weren't?

Looking back on that experience, I'm surprised I didn't resign sooner. It was a highly paid position for me and one that I had wanted for quite some time, so I thought I could stick it out and wait for things to get better. They never did though. In fact, they got worse.

My boss would publicly call us names, point fingers at anyone who did something wrong during staff meetings, and visibly show anger toward our entire staff. You knew how your entire day would start just by the way they entered the office in the morning. In the short time I was there, eleven of our thirty-two employees quit. I was number twelve.

The greatest negative impact was the manner in which this person communicated to us. Of course, what actually came out of their mouth was shockingly unprofessional—at times even hateful. But it was body language, facial expressions, voice raising, and roaming around the office that communicated far more than any message coming from their mouth.

It's unfortunate, but I've never met someone who didn't have a bad boss at some point in their life. It's a tough situation to be in. So, if you're reading this and YOU are the boss, do a quick, honest assessment on yourself and reflect on how you feel your employees would talk about your communication style. Good news is that this chapter can help if you need it!

On the other hand, good communicators are well aware that effective body language often telegraphs an idea ahead of mere words. People who communicate effectively understand that *how* they communicate is just as important as the words others hear.

Are you aware of your body language? Were you thinking about body language the last time you made a presentation or had to confront someone? What about with your next upcoming presentation or group meeting—will you remember the importance of maintaining solid eye contact and controlling your facial expressions and posture? Again, remember that 90 percent of what you communicate is not said verbally but is demonstrated physically via your body language.

> **"The most important thing in communication**
> **is to hear what isn't being said."**
> **— PETER DRUCKER**

Most communication in today's fast-paced society is unspoken, not only because of body language considerations but also because of technology.

Think for a moment about all the ways you communicate on a daily basis. When was the last time you wrote a letter and sent it via the post office? Perhaps you can't even remember.

Traditional stamp-and-envelope mail—or "snail mail" as it is sometimes called these days—has been replaced by a plethora of other communication strategies such as email, text messaging, Facebook, Twitter, LinkedIn, Instagram, and other various social media and app platforms. Think of all the ways in which you have communicated with someone just today alone. Chances are you have used at least a couple of these methods.

Clearly, face-to-face communication these days has given way—sometimes even across a shared dinner table—to the numerous electronic means of "reaching out." At times, it seems we may no longer even need face-to-face interaction.

Certainly, technology has made communication more easy and immediate. But has it made it any more effective? Have we given up clarity and personality in favor of speed and convenience?

Across classrooms, in residence halls, in our homes, and in our offices, we routinely text or instant-message people who may be as close as next door, in the next cubicle, or even in the same room!

But just because we "can" doesn't mean we *always* "should." An email or a text message is not always the most effective or accurate means of communication. There's no denying that almost everyone at some time or another has sent or received an email that has been misunderstood. No wonder today's devices are overpopulated with thousands of emotionally diverse "Smiley Face" emojis. Of necessity, they have become the electronic substitute for body language!

To be effective communicators we must understand that just because we send a message, such as an email, it does not mean we have "communicated" what we intended. We cannot rely on technology to replace conversations that should be taking place in person. We may think we have communicated well when we have not.

**"The single biggest problem in communication
is the illusion that it has taken place."**
— *GEORGE BERNARD SHAW*

Have you heard, or even said, any of the following:

You didn't get my email?
We posted the minutes. You didn't read them?
We sent everyone a message on Facebook.
Your message must have gone to my SPAM.
Our email was down for the day.
You didn't get my text?

These are just a few of the excuses people commonly use for not receiving messages. I have heard every one of them. I've even used a few myself. Sometimes they are the truth; sometimes they are little white lies because we know we can blame technology. After all, who will refute us? And despite the occasional glitch—real or fabricated—no one is going to stop using their email or text messaging service to communicate.

We depend upon technology so much that we have become passive communicators. We send an email and think it's done, that an issue is handled, and that's it for us. But on the other end, perhaps the message really doesn't arrive. Or maybe, due to a slow server somewhere along the line, it arrives too late in the recipient's inbox to be of any help. Or maybe your message was unintentionally overlooked or deleted by the recipient.

The next time you have something very important to communicate, consider all the means by which you can get your message across—not just the ones that involve imper-sonal texting. Consider calling the person directly. If it's about business, maybe arrange a meeting. Meetings don't have to be long, and they can be very effective. My rule of thumb is:

If I have to scroll to read it, I pick up the phone.

Remember, just because you think you have communicated does not mean you actually *have*. Your message or its reply could easily be lost in the ether. And when you are face-to-face, do not forget the messages you communicate in your facial expressions, vocal tone, demeanor, gestures and body language overall. A genuine smile, or lack thereof, communicates a message! Remember, it's not what you say, but how you say it!

Note: My most requested workshop is titled "High Performance Communication!" You can download the PowerPoint and handouts via my website, ***www.KevinCSnyder.com/Resources*** or you can find it at ***www.SlideShare.com*** by searching for "Kevin Snyder and High Performance Communication."

Attitude of Gratitude

"Nothing new can come in your life until you appreciate what you already have."
— MICHAEL BECKWITH

A t the closing of one of my presentations, I share the following message and give out rocks that I call my Gratitude Rocks. If you don't have one of my Gratitude Rocks handy at the moment, just look around you now and identify something nearby that is both tangible and special, something that is symbolic to you. That's the equivalent of your "rock."

Once you have the item in hand, read the following:

Keep this item in a common place, so that every time you see it or touch it, you will be reminded of the many things in your life you can be grateful for. You cannot attract any more into your life until you appreciate what you already have.

Focus on living in abundance and you will attract more of it because you are powerfully attracting more good things to you. It's the Law of Attraction—you become what you think about most; by your thinking, you attract! And gratitude is one of the most powerful forces because appreciating what you already have prepares you to have even more.

The greatest teachers and inventors who have ever lived have told us that the Law of Attraction is the most powerful law. What you focus on, you attract to you. Your focus is like a magnet! This universal Law responds to your thoughts, both positive and negative. Most people think and focus on what they do *not* want, like problems and debt, for example. Then they wonder why these things keep showing up in their lives over and over again. But when you focus on what you want, what you do not want will go away. **You have a power inside you that is waiting to be unleashed at a level beyond your imagination.**

This power has an extraordinary ability to change anything in your life because you are the one who chooses your thoughts. It is a well-known fact that you come to believe whatever you repeat to yourself, whether the statement is true or false. We are what we are because of the dominating thoughts that we *permit* to occupy our mind! So, appreciate what you already have—that's gratitude!

This is your life, and it's been waiting for you to discover it. You deserve it. Yes, you deserve all the good things life has to offer.

"If you think you'll lose, you're lost.

For out of the world we find,

Success begins with a fellow's will.

It's all in the state of mind.

Life's battles don't always go

To the stronger or faster man,

But soon or late the man who wins

Is the one WHO THINKS HE CAN!"

— **WALTER D. WINTEL**

On the next page, write down what you are grateful for. But don't rush this process. Do this at a time when you are focused and have minimal distractions around you. Just like building your vision board, you must also be specific.

For example, don't just write "family." Instead, write down each person's name. Instead of writing, "health," write down what it is about your health you appreciate.

And as you write down what you're grateful for, be aware of how you feel. Recognize the emotion and energy surrounding you. Be mindful of the chills in your body, the smile on your face, and the gratitude you are expressing in your heart.

If you've done this exercise in an undisturbed setting, what's already happening is the Law of Attraction in full effect! Your appreciation and gratitude are energy and you are feeling it. Through this activity, you are magnetically attracting even more of those things to you.

So, if you are just reading and haven't done this exercise, I highly, highly encourage you to take a moment and complete it.

And remember, this process only works for those who believe it will!

The Essence of Survival

Every morning in Africa, a lion wakes up.
It knows it must run faster than the slowest gazelle
or else it will starve to death. Every morning in
Africa, a gazelle wakes up. It knows it must run
faster than the fastest lion or else it will be eaten.
In Africa, it doesn't matter whether you are a lion
or gazelle, because when the sun comes up,
you'd better be running.

This book is about you. This book is about equipping you with ideas that can help make this coming year the best year of your life. This book is also about reminding you and affirming what you already know. The question is, are you applying these concepts to your life?

I believe each of us has an opportunity to make a difference in this world. We have a responsibility to leave this world a better place. To be givers, not takers. We have opportunities every single day to inspire those around us and make people better.

To accomplish this though, and to reach our full potential by doing so, we must *think differently*. And we must *think differently* than most everyone else. Only by *thinking differently* we will become magnificently successful and feel fulfilled along the journey.

What role will you play in this world? Will you be a lion or will you be a gazelle?

I believe we all want to be lions, but sometimes we make gazelle decisions. We all want to make a difference, but we act indifferent. We all want to have more, but we don't appreciate what we already have.

You could be a seasoned corporate executive or "just" a young student.

You could be president of a company or "just" an employee holding no official position at all.

You could be the leader of a team or "just" a team member.

You could be a school principal or "just" a caring math teacher like my mom and sister.

You're not really "just" anything. You are who you are with the opportunity to make an extraordinary impact in this world. With a think differently mindset,
YOU ARE A LION,
regardless of your position or circumstance!

IT'S TIME TO HEAR YOUR ROAR!

On a lighter note, each of us has something in our life we would like to change or be different. But for that change to begin, we must understand our role in making that change. Change starts with action, not intention.

Every chapter you have read in this book contains a message of how to unleash your personal power. The common denominator of every chapter in this book is the idea and opportunity that passion, commitment, sacrifice, and an unwavering positive attitude can, together, attract everything you want in life.

"Know what you want. Believe you deserve it.
Take persistent action until it shows up in your life.
Celebrate but never become complacent."
— KEVIN C. SNYDER

THINK DIFFERENTLY!

Motivation Matters

SHORT LEADERSHIP STORIES AND QUOTES FOR YOUR TEAM

Diamonds Are Only Made By Pressure

Do you know how diamonds are actually formed? Read this; it will change your perception.

The word "diamond" is derived from the Greek word *adamos*, meaning the unconquerable. Diamond is one of the strongest and most chemically inert materials on Earth. It is nearly impossible to break, and it can withstand the attack of nearly any chemical. Natural diamonds are produced deep under the Earth's crust under conditions of high temperature and high pressure.

This story explaining the creation of the diamond should remind us how life's pressure can make us stronger, more beautiful people. We cannot produce diamonds without first understanding our own natural qualities and overcoming life's frustrations. The pressure we experience also creates who we are and who we will become.

Perhaps there is a diamond of opportunity hidden in a difficulty you're experiencing right now. It may not be a diamond yet but be patient; it is forming within you.

— *KEVIN C. SNYDER*

The Seven Up's

1. Wake Up! Focus on something you look forward to in the day ahead.

2. Dress Up! The best way to dress up is to put on a smile. A smile is an inexpensive way to improve your looks.

3. Shut Up! Say nice things and learn to listen. We have two ears and one mouth for a reason.

4. Stand Up! For what you believe in. Stand for something or you will fall for anything.

5. Show Up! Opportunities are never lost. They're just passed on to someone else.

6. Reach Up! For your goals, dreams and aspirations. Expect you will achieve them.

7. Lift Up! Be grateful for what you do have. Nothing new can come into your life until you appreciate what you already have.

— *KEVIN C. SNYDER*

The Power
To Really Live

I like what Mark Twain said about enthusiasm. When asked the reason for his success, he replied, "I was born excited."

The happiest, most fulfilled, and most successful people have discovered the necessity of an enthusiastic approach to living. Thomas Edison was also such a person. He was known for his energy and verve. He eventually acquired 1,093 patents for his inventions, including the electric light bulb, phonograph, and motion picture camera. He was known to work tirelessly and joyfully. He seemed to have loved what he did, and he pursued his work with passion. Others have made more money than Thomas Edison, but none have been more enthusiastic or productive.

Ralph Waldo Emerson once said, "Enthusiasm is one of the most powerful engines of success. When you do a thing, do it with all your might. Put your whole soul into it. Stamp it with your own personality. Be active, be energetic, be enthusiastic and faithful, and you will accomplish your objective." Enthusiasm is an engine fueled by a love for what we do. It will power us anywhere we want to go and take us places we would never reach without it!

What are you enthusiastic about? What do you desire?

— *KEVIN C. SNYDER*

Achieving
Your Dreams

**"It's not what you are that holds you back.
It's what you think you're not." — Denis Waitley**

Those wise words from Denis Waitley probably explain more about people's failure to achieve the life they seek than any other quote I've read. What keeps most people from achieving their dreams is they spend too much time dwelling on their weaknesses and shortcomings instead of focusing on their gifts. That's significantly due to their self-esteem or lack thereof. Remember, you get what you focus on. And what you focus on expands.

— *KEVIN C. SNYDER*

The Road To Success
Is Not Straight

There is a curve called Failure, a loop called Confusion, speed bumps called Friends, red lights called Enemies, exits called Temptation, caution lights called Family, and possibly flat tires called Jobs.

But if you have a spare tire called Determination, an engine called Persistence, a map called Strategy, insurance called Faith, and a driver called Passion, you will arrive at your destination called SUCCESS!

— *T.E. BOYD*

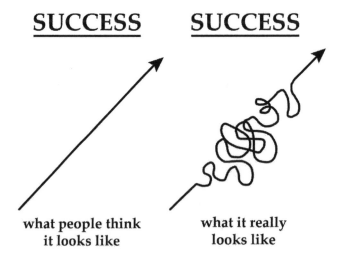

SUCCESS   SUCCESS

what people think   what it really
it looks like   looks like

Everybody, Somebody, Anybody, and Nobody

This is a little story about four people named Everybody, Somebody, Anybody, and Nobody.

There was an important job to be done and Everybody was sure that Somebody would do it.

Anybody could have done it, but Nobody did it.

Somebody got angry about that because it was Everybody's job.

Everybody thought that Anybody could do it, but Nobody realized that Everybody wouldn't do it.

It ended up that Everybody blamed Somebody when Nobody did what Anybody could have done.

— *ANONYMOUS*

The Power Of Giving

Whatever you want more of, try giving it away.

You want more time? *Volunteer.*
You want better knowledge? *Give away some books.*
You want better relationships? *Be a great friend.*
Want more money? *Donate money to someone who really needs it.*

What you sow, you'll reap. What does a farmer do? He plants a seed and a harvest is created. Take an inventory of what you have to give away. What about a smile, insight, time, or money. Stop holding on tight and start opening up and putting yourself in the FLOW of life—giving and receiving. It makes the world go round.

What are your talents, gifts, and skills? How do you share them? Do you "give" them away?

— *KEVIN C. SNYDER*

Quotes

"Somebody is always doing what somebody else said couldn't be done." — *AUTHOR UNKNOWN*

"In the middle of every difficulty lies opportunity—once discovered, such opportunities are like valuable diamonds hidden in the sand." — *ALBERT EINSTEIN*

"When we long for life without difficulties, remind us that oaks grow strong in contrary winds and diamonds are made under pressure." — *AUTHOR UNKNOWN*

"Try to be a rainbow in someone's cloud."
— *MAYA ANGELOU*

"Happiest are the people who give most happiness to others." — *DENNIS DIDEROT, PHILOSOPHER*

"Start by doing what's necessary; then do what's possible; and suddenly you are doing the impossible."
— *FRANCIS OF ASSISI*

"No one has a right to consume happiness without producing it." — *HELEN KELLER, AMERICAN AUTHOR AND LECTURER*

"What would you do differently if you knew you could not fail?" — *ROBERT H. SCHULLER*

"If you want happiness for an hour—take a nap.
If you want happiness for a day—go fishing.
If you want happiness for a year—inherit a fortune.
If you want happiness for a lifetime—help someone else."
— CHINESE PROVERB

"You don't have to get it right, you just have to get it going."
— MIKE LITMAN

"The more you seek security, the less of it you have. But the more you seek opportunity, the more likely it is that you will achieve the security that you desire." *— BRIAN TRACY*

Happiness & Success Thoughts

Happiness can be caught, sought, or thought,
but never bought. — *UNKNOWN*

The best way to keep happiness is to share it. — *UNKNOWN*

Happiness is not created by what happens to us, but by
our attitudes toward each happening. — *UNKNOWN*

It isn't our position but our disposition
which makes us happy. — *UNKNOWN*

Stopping at third base adds nothing to the score.
— *BILLY SUNDAY*

That lucky rabbit's foot didn't work for the rabbit.
— *UNKNOWN*

Even a woodpecker owes his success to the fact that he
uses his head. — *COLEMAN COX*

Anywhere is paradise; it's up to you to see it. — *UNKNOWN*

Happiness is a slice of life—buttered. — *UNKNOWN*

If you think you can or you think you can't, you're right!
— *HENRY FORD*

My Wish

I wish you will know how it feels "to run" with all your heart and then lose ... horribly.

I wish that you will achieve some great good for mankind that no one knows about except you.

I wish you will find something so worthwhile that it makes you come alive and desire to invest your life pursuing it.

I hope you become so frustrated and challenged that you want to quit. I hope you don't quit though because you'll be pushing through the barriers of your own limitations.

I hope you make a stupid mistake and get caught red-handed and are big enough to say those three magic words: "I was wrong."

I hope you give so much of yourself that some days, just some days, you wonder if it's worth all the effort.

I wish for you a magnificent obsession that will give you purpose and direction and a reason to wake up each morning.

I wish for you naysayers and criticism for whatever

you do, because that makes you fight to achieve more than you otherwise might have done.

I sincerely wish you all to have the experience of thinking a new idea, planning it, organizing it, and following it to completion, and then having it be magnificently successful.

I WISH FOR YOU
THE EXPERIENCE OF LEADERSHIP.

Simple Truths of Leadership

Leadership is about **action**,
not position.

Leadership is about **transformation**,
not transaction.

Leadership is about **influence**,
not management.

Leadership *is a* **verb**,
not a noun.

— *KEVIN C. SNYDER*

• *BEFORE YOU GO* •

Before you go, send me an email

and tell me what you thought about this book:

Kevin@KevinCSnyder.com.

Also tweet & post your thoughts to

#ThinkDifferently and

@KevinCSnyder

Let me send you a special link to download my FREE leadership resources!

Thank you for investing your valuable time to read *Think Differently*! Since we're of "like mind," I'd like to send you a special free link to download many of my leadership resources. Simply visit **www.KevinCSnyder.com** and enter your email address when the opt-in image appears. You'll receive an immediate response with the special link.

You are welcome to send me a message—via email, social media, website, or my app. Share your thoughts, your struggles, or your new-found strengths. I'd be honored to hear from you.

After you finish reading *Think Differently*, please share a testimonial and help spread the positive message of this book to others! I'd love to read your thoughts. Submit your testimonial on Amazon.com following these easy steps:

#1: *Visit www.Amazon.com*

#2: *In the Amazon search bar, type "Think Differently" and "Kevin Snyder" so that you find this book. Click on it!*

#3: *Scroll down and click on "Write a Customer Review." Add your review and submit it!*

#4: *After writing your review, email me at Kevin@KevinCSnyder.com and I will reply with an additional special link for FREE stuff!*

Note: Although Amazon.com is preferred, you can also visit my website to make book purchases, leave reviews (***www.KevinCSnyder.com***) or contact me directly for bulk discount orders (***Kevin@KevinCSnyder.com***)

A bit more about the author, Kevin Snyder

D r. Kevin Snyder is a motivational speaker and author with a PASSION for helping individuals and organizations empower themselves and others. Visit his website at *www.KevinCSnyder.com* for more free leadership resources, to download this book, and inquire about him speaking for your next event.

Through his motivational speaking career, Kevin has presented for over 500,000 people, over 1,150 audiences in all 50 states and numerous countries.

Kevin speaks to high schools, colleges, professional organizations and associations of all types. He is also the founder of *Empower YOUth!,* a youth leadership program for school assemblies, teacher in-service events, district personnel trainings, and student leadership conferences.

DYNAMIC LEADERSHIP PRESENTATIONS FOR STUDENTS AND EDUCATORS

Kevin has taught at the high school, community college, and university level. Prior to becoming a professional speaker, Kevin held a career in Student Affairs and most recently served as the Dean of Students for High Point University. Prior to HPU, he served the University of Central Florida as the Director for the College of Education. He also worked at Embry-Riddle Aeronautical University and the University of South Carolina. Kevin's Masters and Doctorate degrees are both in Educational Leadership.

As a published author and speaker, Kevin also coaches aspiring authors and speakers to meet their writing and speaking goals.

Kevin is a Forbes magazine contributor, a former staff member aboard Semester at Sea, a sailboat charter captain, a certified skydiver, scuba diver, kiteboarding enthusiast, and most interestingly, a winner on television's most famous game show, *The Price Is Right!*

To learn more about Kevin and his presentations, please visit his website:

www.KevinCSnyder.com

Motivation Matters!

I would love to stay in touch!

Subscribe to my motivational e-newsletter and receive a weekly motivational message. Visit www.KevinCSnyder. com to subscribe. On my website, you can also download a free copy of this book to share with others!

Follow me on your social of choice
@KevinCSnyder

BONUS!

Even more

Also, receive your "Daily Dose" motivational quote by downloading my leadership app!

KevinCSnyder

Are you interested in speaking?

*Curious what it takes to become
a professional speaker?*

I've written a book where I share it all!

PURCHASE

HOW TO BECOME A PROFESSIONAL SPEAKER:
PAID To SPEAK!

via Amazon

Visit my website for free
speaker resources on building
a speaking business and
to contact me for a free
30-minute coaching call:
www.PAIDtoSPEAK.biz

*... teaching speakers how to build a
successful, PAID speaking business!*

PAIDtoSPEAK.biz

Are you interested in writing a book?

*Curious what it takes to become
a published author?*

*Download your FREE eBook,
"How to Write a Book in 90 Days!"*

Visit *www.WriteWayPublishingCompany.com*

*Tell us more about your book concept and we'll tell you
exactly what you need to do in order to get it published*!

Made in the USA
Columbia, SC
13 March 2019